The King of Bullsh*t News ?

By Michael Leidig

Copyright © 2024 by CEN Ltd / Michael Leidig.

First published in Great Britain in 2024 by CEN Ltd.

This edition (1.0) was published in April 2024.

The right of Michael Leidig to be identified as the owner of this work has been asserted by him in accordance with the Copyright, Designs and Patents Act 1988.

This book is a public document. A CIP catalogue record for this title is available from the British Library.

Every effort has been made to ensure accuracy, but in the event of a request for
editorial corrections, please write to: editor@cen.at

Cover art by Zorica Stojkovik, CEN: (https://shorturl.at/imDW6)

Dedication

This book is about the dangers of what happens when the media strays from a path laid down by the legendary *Guardian* editor C.P. Scott when he said: *"The voice of opponents no less than that of friends has a right to be heard."* It is to remind those who should care about journalism, from *BuzzFeed* to the *Guardian,* of the dangers of straying and as a warning for those who are worried about the future of our profession and the future in general. It is dedicated to those who feature in these pages that kept us in business, including Patrick Masters from the *Sunday Times Insight* team, Paul Halloran, who was *Private Eye's* former Senior Investigative Reporter and the first full-time journalist they ever employed, and my long-suffering lawyer Harry Wise, as well as *Press Gazette* editor Dominic Ponsford for standing up for the underdog, despite the legal challenges he faced, proving the truth of what Oscar Wilde said: *"Speaking the truth that somebody wants you not to publish is journalism. Everything else is marketing."* It's also for my colleagues, including Rob Hyde, Dan Harrison, Darko Manevski and Ana Marjanovic, as well as proofreaders Marija Stojkoska, Angela Trajkovska, and Joe Golder. My friend Michelle Murphy gets a special mention for the daily phone calls and support, and last but not least, my long-suffering family of Natie, MJ and my wife Violeta, who have had enough of being in the media spotlight, and despite the jibes of being related to "The King Of Bullsh*t News", have helped me to stay the course.

* * *

Contents

CHAPTER ONE – THE 5 W's AND ONE H 6
    Who What, Where, When, Why and How The F*** It Happened? 6

CHAPTER TWO - PUBLISH AND BE DAMNED 8
    Don't Talk To Me About Infamy, They've All Got It Infamy 8

CHAPTER THREE - THE KING 12
    His Royal Slyness 12

CHAPTER FOUR - SECRET AGENTS 20
    Trade Craft 20
    The End of the Beginning 24

CHAPTER FIVE - FACECROOKS 26
    Anti Social 26

CHAPTER SIX - MAIL ORDER 41
    Post Mortem Slackers 41

CHAPTER SEVEN - SOMETHING ROTTEN IN THE STATES 50
    Fake View 50

CHAPTER EIGHT - GOING NATIVE 56
    Ads Your Lot 56
    Smith Of Scandal 64

CHAPTER NINE - HERE IS THE NEWS 66
    Cabbages And King 66
    Vegging Out 66
    Pretty In Pink Kittens 67
    Bed And Bawdy 69
    Sashimi Tapeworm 70
    You Have To Be Kidding 71

CHAPTER TEN - PUBLISH AND BE SLAMMED 73
    Vocal Recall 73
    Traffic Jammed 90

CHAPTER ELEVEN - BUZZ OFFED 95
    Newsfakers 95

CHAPTER TWELVE - WAY TO GO 101
    NewsX ™ 101

AND FINALLY 103
    Appendix Of Documents 104

CHAPTER ONE – THE 5 W's AND ONE H

Who What, Where, When, Why and How The F*** It Happened?

These are the questions that should be at the heart of any piece of journalism, like this book, for example. As with many things that don't go as you expect, I did not set out to write a book while answering them. I was only making notes for my New York-based lawyer, Harry Wise, explaining how the English media landscape worked so he could fight a libel case for me against the online site for Top 10 lists BuzzFeed.

You know the one, if you want to know about 'People Who Get Horny Watching Game of Thrones', that's the place to be. They had accused me and my small, Vienna-based news agency of being what they described as 'The King of Bullsh*t News'. As I maintained this allegation was a complete fabrication, that they then refused to correct or change, I had assumed it would be easy to get the courts to do this for me. I was wrong.

In the UK, the media has to prove the truth of what it writes when challenged; in America, it's the other way around. The court eventually decided that the untimely death of our Russian correspondent and the unavailability of a part-time Chinese stringer who had written three stories meant we could not prove our case, and so BuzzFeed won, even though there was no evidence showing any story had ever been falsified by me, or my reporting team.

But as the various stages of the legal process were being chronicled in my notes, I realised that my apparent fall from grace was a microcosm of what's been happening in the broader media landscape. It taught me lessons I was able to apply to my editorial team. Lessons that would help us operate in the new media landscape where allegations like those that BuzzFeed had made were becoming all too common and, in turn, offer lessons to be learned if we are to fix it.

The reality is that there is still good journalism, but for every genuine article produced by what is now referred to as legacy media, hundreds of thousands of stories are being created that are designed to look like journalism but have nothing to do with it.

Earlier this month, while investigating a smear campaign spreading around the web, I found news sites that boasted of publishing 10,000 'news' stories an hour, with no journalists. Against that, my agency, with 30 staff, typically manages around 50 stories daily. It's easy to guess which site with no reporters at all, and with its content 100% provided by PR and marketing firms, has the coveted 'Google News' status and which does not. It's easy also to guess which site gets paid a large amount for every single story they publish with no work, and which is paid for only one in four articles. You guessed it, my team is the one that gets the rough end of the deal. But until we start treating journalists and media organisations that invest in journalists properly, this will not change.

So although my immediate circle of friends, family and colleagues believe that 'The King of Bullsh*t News' is old news, and that I should finally drop the subject, pointing out that nobody will be interested, I have continued to disagree, and have put together this summarised narrative in the belief others will share my point of view. I also believe that the main reason this story is so remarkable is that the exact same people who were so intimately involved in what happened to me were also those who I would argue, more than any others, are to blame for the disastrous state of the media today: Ben Smith and Jonah Peretti.

Together, they helped create the terrible polarisation that has destroyed societies; they moulded and shaped the attitudes of social media giants, encouraging them by their actions and whispered words to introduce controls on news production that then affected everybody else, they hoovered up hundreds of millions in funding which was squandered on largely worthless content, and cynically sprinkled it with a handful of serious news stories to give some credibility to the manipulations and vested interest narratives they published as news.

But above all their terrible mistakes, more than anyone else, they were the ones that were responsible for breaking down the separation between church and state, allowing advertising, which has nothing to do with journalism, to flood onto the news pages. They then tried to blame everybody else afterwards for the devastation they had caused.

So, despite those who think it might be better just to move on, I believe that it's only by reporting this that lessons can be learned, and a good way to start doing that is by answering this question: Who is really 'The King of Bullsh*t News'?

Is it me?

Or is it BuzzFeed?

* * *

CHAPTER TWO - PUBLISH AND BE DAMNED

Don't Talk To Me About Infamy, They've All Got It Infamy

You need a thick skin and a good lawyer to be a journalist, at least if you're going to do the job correctly. Oscar Wilde summed it up best when he said: "Speaking the truth that somebody wants you not to publish is journalism. Everything else is marketing." In my career, I have constantly been upsetting somebody somewhere in some corner of the world, and while my list of media partners is like a Who's Who of the world's media, I sometimes feel the legal firms that have either worked for me or against me is like a Who's Who of the global legal landscape.

I am not alone, and it is the many problems like this that are why, almost every year, journalism is voted the worst job in the world. The organisation Career Cast cites "Dwindling employment opportunities, poor pay and routine exposure to hazardous conditions . . ." as top among the many reasons journalism is awarded the infamous number one spot with alarming regularity. More than 120 journalists were recorded dead in action last year alone (2023).

It's been like that for as long as I can remember. When considering my career path, my university had a dusty archive where former students could leave reviews about the advantages and disadvantages of the jobs they had later chosen. Most of the sections were full of detailed notes from alumni, and among the many choices, there was also one, and only one, for journalism. The handwritten note advised students considering the career that if they chose journalism, they could give up on any idea of a social life. The hours are long and the pay is poor compared to other professions. To get a foothold, you often have to work for free for weeks or months to be considered for a newsroom position. The fact that there was only this one review for journalism while the folders for other careers like PR or marketing were bursting at the seams was testimony to the truth of those words.

My friend Jon Harris, who runs the Manchester-based British news agency Cavendish Press, told me recently that his daughter can earn more babysitting than he can as a senior reporter. And a journalism professor at Syracuse University in New York tweeted a picture of the "Now Hiring" sign from the popular burger chain Five Guys on his campus. It offered paid work at $17.85 per hour, significantly more than most of the graduates who ate food there could hope to make in local TV news.

The conditions most journalists have to work under are not conducive to doing the job correctly. I can't say I was not warned precisely how it would be when I read the fading review of the profession as an undergraduate and went into it anyway, and here I am, three decades later, living proof that every word of it was true. If you asked why I do it, and don't take the tempting offers from the dark side to go into PR and marketing, I would struggle to find a single answer. Yet I am reminded of the old adage "Find something you love and you'll never have to work a day in your life". I went into journalism to satisfy an endless curiosity, and while many careers can kill a passion, journalism has only strengthened mine, fostering a desire to know and then to share.

When I briefly escaped from the treadmill to a well-paid job as a news presenter for a radio station in Vienna, I was welcomed at red-carpet events and VIP parties and paid a fortune for working only a handful of days every month, but I got bored. After two years, and with a bulging bank account, I resigned and launched my news agency in Austria, allowing me to write what I wanted, not what anyone else told me to write. The stories we covered were as wide as the interests of the specialist magazines and newspapers we worked for. As a result, though small, my new agency, Central European News, or CEN for short, has always punched above its weight, with its core rooted in principles that define quality news reporting.

In fact, very early on, we were invited to be part of the respected UK organisation, the National Association Of Press Agencies (NAPA), where I am now the vice chairman. I oversee special projects at NAPA, looking for ways to fund what we do without compromising our values. It has not been easy. In fact, I thought I'd had it tough when I started out and was willing to pay that price. But when you think that things can't get any worse, life can surprise you, and they do.

Of course, what I didn't know was that at the beginning of 2014, across the pond in New York, the then CFO of BuzzFeed, Mark Frackt, who was also the CEO of BuzzFeed UK, was in discussions that 16 months later would result in the publication of The King Of Bullsh*t News, and after that a campaign to try and close me down by an editorial team of people that I had never met working in the city I was born in, London. The BuzzFeed UK team at the time had also never done an investigation, and those taking on the challenge had previously cut their teeth by drawing up lists like '37 Things That Will Make You Grin Like A Buffoon'. Not exactly Watergate.

Slowly this dialogue that began with Frackt, who had joined BuzzFeed in 2011, then widened to include more of BuzzFeed's senior management. On the back of that, BuzzFeed's editor-in-chief, Ben Smith, chose the headline that was to define me for the next decade, the headline that is also the title of this book, and that accused me of running a global fake news factory. It didn't matter that he had no evidence it was true when he passed it on to his minions, and it didn't matter that he still had no evidence when it was published; he remains unrepentant.

Asked if he was the one who authorised publication, he replied: "Ultimately, yes. The buck stops at me. It's my decision." He and his team did not just accuse me of running any old fake news factory. As he was not worried about having any proof, imagination was the only limit to his ambition, so Ben Smith made me the boss, the king, the ruler of the greatest fake news factory of them all. The BuzzFeed story then continued the devastating work of the headline:

" . . . the evidence assembled by BuzzFeed News suggests that an alarming proportion of CEN's 'weird news' stories are based on exaggeration, embellishment, and outright fabrication . . . "

" . . . the company has scant regard either for the accuracy of its content - or for what happens to the people whose names and images are spread across the world."

" The questionable nature of CEN's content has become something of an open secret among online news and picture desk editors . . . "

The allegations were big talk for an organisation that was also telling its readers 'You Might Be Cleaning Your Penis Wrong'. I hated the BuzzFeed headline about me at the time, but I've since learned to think about it, shall we say, differently. Time and time again, each attempt in the fight to have this ludicrous lie corrected or taken down ended in frustration. It's true that at the end of each round, I was still the King to the outside world.

But each time, I picked myself up and started again, and again, and after a while, something transformational began to happen. Although it was still painful on a personal level, their headline no longer had the same power to harm my business. Their one weapon had misfired, which meant I was free to fight back. Like the law of double jeopardy, where you can only be punished once, in a weird way, I had become bulletproof, too.

When BuzzFeed decided to create the story about me, an investigations unit had been set up in London, UK, for one purpose, and one purpose only: to prove that I was everything they claimed, that I was the King that Ben Smith had decreed. And as sure as night follows day, a story was produced under the headline 'The King of Bullsh*t News'.

As far as I know, it was the first and only story that the team ever produced. And there may be a good reason for that. Not only was it complete bullsh*t itself, but it was also the first falling pebble in the landslide that eventually engulfed BuzzFeed as a force in news.

There was nothing of truth in Ben Smith's fever dream headline or the story that followed. In fact, everything in it had simply been cut and pasted from the Internet despite the huge cast of so-called investigators.

It offended me on so many levels. It is, of course, horrific to be the epicentre of such venom and spite and someone trying to pull down your life's work. But even in the centre of this maelstrom, you remain a pro, and it was just downright insulting to be attacked in a piece of such shabbily cobbled-together rumours and speculation.

If they'd bothered to do any research, any at all, into the too-good-to-be-true CEN stories they had declared to be fiction, they would have found they were true. Even where there were problems, they did not lie at my door. It was something they were to learn later to their cost. Anyone in this business more than the five minutes of Ben Smith's BuzzFeed knows that the world is plenty weird enough without having to make anything up.

The only thing that their UK team, which had recruited Heidi Blake from the Sunday Times Insight team as its head, knew for sure was that we were beating them in the business of viral news and selling it to their rivals, as evidenced by some of the information I was to glean from the early BuzzFeed discussions about me.

Frequent links to MailOnline, particularly, were notching up viral hits with the content we supplied. As BuzzFeed sought a solid reader base in the UK, it eyed these numbers hungrily. But, of course, that couldn't possibly have been a motive, could it?

The fact that the allegations that they were to later make had the potential to kick holes in their competitors, like MailOnline, was just BuzzFeed doing responsible journalism, wasn't it? The strange thing about this is that the headline is usually only written after the story is done, because journalism does need to be responsible. If you are going to claim something, you need to know it's true, right?

You don't need to watch a Spider-Man movie to know that with great power comes great responsibility. And when you work as a journalist and for the biggest names in the business, that is great power. But despite this responsibility, the BuzzFeed investigations team didn't find it strange that they had the headline first and were told to make it a reality. After all, they were high on the idea that they might be doing some real journalism.

They wanted an end to the mindless drudgery of '17 People Who Got Unspeakably Horny Due To Game Of Thrones', and there are only so many times you can draw a huge phallus on the front page of the Sun and post it online where people still find it funny. These are, by the way, real examples of what passed for journalism by members of BuzzFeed's crack investigation team before they started writing about me.

* * *

CHAPTER THREE - THE KING

His Royal Slyness

The BuzzFeed headline was a damning title, and the 'story' underneath that headline, with its one-sided dialogue, continued the online assault. It had been put together by wordsmiths like Heidi Blake and the Pulitzer Prize winner Mark Schoofs, who were undoubtedly masters of the art of storytelling, and I realised that there would be no happy ending for me as I read its contents on that day of infamy.

It was a Saturday, and the day had all seemed so different moments earlier. I was about to have friends around to celebrate my 50th birthday. I had a pledge of at least half a million euros in seed money to kick-start my Fourth Estate Project. It was the culmination of decades in journalism where I planned to build something that could fill the void for content in struggling newsrooms. Something that could make a difference in providing real news and not simply chasing traffic with clickbait or cut-and-paste journalism.

It was an investment I hoped would allow an escape from a 12-hour plus working day, six days a week, replacing it with something that left time for myself and my family. My nephew George used to joke that when he was a junior doctor, I was the only person he knew who worked longer hours than he did. Yet, with success just a heartbeat away and my friends on their way to my home bearing gifts, I was relaxing when the phone rang in my hallway on my way to the garden.

I was balancing a pot of tea and a plate of toast but somehow managed to answer the phone anyway. It was a call from Allan Hall, a now-retired freelance journalist based in Berlin, who was both a rival for the German news market, a colleague, and a friend. He'd asked me if I'd seen the news, which had just been sent to him by another correspondent, Peter Allen, in Paris.

When it became clear I didn't know what he was talking about; he told me an article had been written about me and my agency. Then I knew what he was talking about, and when I searched the story on my phone and saw the headline, my hopes and dreams vanished as if they had never been anything other than a morning mist, fleeting - and quickly forgotten.

I couldn't bring myself to read the rest of what was written underneath the headline. Instead, I walked into the garden holding my phone, pale, in a zombie-like trance. My wife realised something was wrong. I didn't reply when she asked what had happened. I simply handed her the phone with the BuzzFeed article open on the screen, and told her as she read it: "I think my career's over."

I didn't see any point in continuing in journalism. I'd had an inkling that BuzzFeed might be writing something, but I'd never imagined anything of this scale. Their reporter Alan White had been calling me claiming he wanted to report on our award-winning journalism, something his boss Heidi Blake had told him would get him into the newsroom for a sit-down chat.

When the BuzzFeed team had cut and pasted as many negative stories about me and CEN as they could from the Internet, instead of checking if the allegations were true by going to the places where the stories happened and speaking to the people involved, they opted for the much easier route of asking me to point out the flaws in their work. And, of course, with Heidi Blake, whose specialisation was the sleazy business of entrapment journalism dictating the strategy, they did not call me directly and ask if the online allegations were true. Instead, they attempted to gain the information they wanted through subterfuge.

The first call from Alan White boiled down to: "Hello Mr Leidig, Alan White. I am from BuzzFeed News. You have a great agency, and congratulations on all the work you're doing. I think how you fund serious investigative journalism from a tabloid news feed is fantastic. I would love to fly over to Vienna to meet you and do a focus story on your agency."

I have to say that from the start, the offer seemed strange to me, given that he rejected out of hand my suggestion that he look for a different NAPA agency that was more interested in being in the spotlight than we were. As we work B2B, with our company website at that time long since mothballed and forgotten, it was a sign that we saw no advantage in promoting what we do to the wider public, and although I suppose many might have responded to the praise with a 'yes', from me, it was a clear 'no'.

I knew immediately that Heidi Blake was probably Alan White's boss if he was working at BuzzFeed, although I must admit I had assumed the enquiry probably came from her praising our journalism. Although unwanted, I reasoned this spotlight treatment was based on our work on child trafficking for the Sunday Times Insight team. I was a little suspicious, but it didn't occur to me in that first call that they were looking at the opposite of his stated intentions. It was just luck for me that he chose the wrong way to open the door by flattering my ego, and I said clearly and without doubt, 'no thanks'.

Hoping to get an interview with a journalist by citing their fame is more likely to work with broadcast journalists, who often really are famous, and therefore more used to being interviewed in reverent tones about their work. However, in contrast, print journalists, with often not even a byline to connect the reporter with the story, are far more anonymous, which is why print is the only type of journalism I enjoy. Print is more about the story and less about the journalist. When we do get them, our bylines are usually ignored by the general public, and the only people who read them are the people who count, usually other journalists or the people involved in the subject matter. I much prefer this arrangement, as in my experience, celebrity journalism does little to advance the quality of what is produced. When my work for the Sunday Telegraph won a Paul Foot Award, arguably the highest accolade in journalism in the UK, I was invited to attend, but I declined. I had other stories to do, so I sent one of my reporters instead.

That was why the BuzzFeed request fell flat; I regarded it as a waste of time and something that would have no useful value. I had no interest in becoming a celebrity journalist, and I never submitted my material for awards. However, that does not mean I don't value what we do in all of its forms, from viral news to in-depth investigations.

And my reply to Alan wasn't just a polite no, it was a categorical 'don't waste my time because I'm not interested', which made me instantly suspicious when he followed up with the following email request:

"From: Alan White [mailto:alan.white@BuzzFeed.com]
Sent: Donnerstag, 02. April 2015 10:02
To: CEN Editor
Subject: Follow up interview

Dear Michael,

Thanks so much for your time yesterday – I really enjoyed chatting to you – and would be really pleased to continue our conversation. The idea behind our piece is to explore the challenges of reporting in the digital age in depth, and how the appetite for quick-fire viral news can end up starving serious journalism of oxygen. I'm particularly interested in the way you manage that mix, because our chat made it clear to me that you're trying to do important, challenging investigative journalism while at the same time producing a very high volume of lighter viral or tabloid stories. I'm hugely interested in how that balance works, and I'd love to talk to you about it some more. I was especially struck by your mention of your lengthy investigation into child trafficking and your failure so far to secure funding for it, and also the mention you made of women's rights in Turkey and child abuse in China - these are exactly the things that the current online ecosystem seems to make it harder and less rewarding to do. CEN seems to be a really interesting example of taking quirky stories from across the world and turning them around quickly for a Western audience, and then using the proceeds (as you say) to fund more substantial investigations."

He then mentions pitfalls in fast turnaround news stories that occasionally do not work. He repeated his offer to fly to Vienna, underlying the fact that money was no obstacle when it came to his CEN story. And at the end, he signed it "Alan", when in fact it should have been signed by "Heidi" who had really written it.

Two things struck me about the email. The first was that the person writing the email, Alan White, didn't understand the basics of journalism. He asked for the interview, and the instant reply was no. Because BuzzFeed was a customer, and I knew Heidi Blake, I made a few extra off-the-record comments, making it clear these were off-the-record, and I found these quoted back at me in his email. Off-the-record is the point in an interview between a journalist and the possible subject of a story where they get to say something without worrying that it will be quoted back at them. It does involve an element of trust and mutual respect, and is therefore more commonly used when a journalist has some personal connection to the person being contacted. They can then say: "Off the record, what's going on here?" It allows a contact to give a reporter an idea if they are on the right track or will need to go in a different direction without the risk of being quoted. I knew Heidi, so that was what I did. It was simply unheard of in my experience that what I had told him off the record, in confidence, should be written down in an email and posted back with the request that I expand on it. He was basically totally clueless.

The second thing was that when it came to paying for stories, BuzzFeed pleaded poverty, but when it came to this story about my largely unknown agency, the budget to fly to Vienna was no problem. This conflict was an irony seemingly lost on Alan White and the rest of the investigations team, but not on their readers if the comments are anything to go by. When the story BuzzFeed wrote about CEN finally appeared, one of the posts underneath was from Jane Hobson, who wrote:

"Pay peanuts, BuzzFeed, get monkeys. $50 a story does not cover the cost of production of either the words or the pictures. What the heck did you think you were getting for that? It's organisations like you that are killing journalism and photojournalism. Quality costs for a reason. And the people who create that quality work are freelance. So you are making professionals redundant, whilst allowing the unprofessional to reign. Shame on you."

For me, though, back in Vienna, despite my clear no to his enquiry, Alan had not got the message and continued calling to the point when he rang me while I was in the car taking my kids to the park, and I was forced to point out that it was getting to the point of harassment. I also reminded him that I had told him repeatedly there would be no interview.

It can't have been anything too aggressive as, despite my annoyance, I was aware my two children were in the car, but it seems to have unsettled Alan White, who told his employers he feared violence if he still came here to confront me.

In an email on 12 April 2015, when the BuzzFeed team discussed Alan's request to move to contacting me via letter rather than going to Vienna, BuzzFeed UK boss Luke Lewis told Alan White that the letter looks solid, but adds: "What are the arguments against going to speak to him in person?" Alan White then replies: ". . . purely personal safety. We are telling him we are about to destroy a business that took him over a decade to build along with his entire professional credibility. You just do not know how a person will react to being put in that situation, nor who he knows out there. If that sounds overcautious so be it, I've ended up in a bad situation before when I thought there was no risk at all."

So CEN staff go to war zones, unravel dangerous criminal networks trafficking arms, women and children, front up corrupt politicians, and track down former Nazi child killers, yet Alan, in his first investigation, is afraid to visit a newsroom in Vienna.[1] With none of the others prepared to fly to Vienna either and risk facing my apparent wrath, BuzzFeed finally had to come clean.

They admitted what they were really up to by sending a long, rambling "front up" letter demanding answers for my shoddy journalism. They wrote: "I wanted to confirm that, as a result of our reporting (sic), BuzzFeed News is now preparing to publish an article which proposes to report that your news agency, CEN, is responsible for the circulation of a string of stories that have subsequently been proven false either in part or in their entirety.

"As I have mentioned previously, I understand that you are producing this viral content for sale in order to fund your laudable investigative journalism, such as your report into the issue of child trafficking in Europe, and I am keen to reflect this fact in the article.

---

[1] *BuzzFeed*_010286 (Subject: 'No surprises letter' – ALAN WHITE, LUKE LEWIS, TOM PHILLIPS, CRAIG SILVERMAN, HEIDI BLAKE,) *

"In the course of our research, we have uncovered numerous substantive inaccuracies and distortions in CEN content which has been sold on to other outlets around the world. We intend to report on this pattern as a matter of legitimate public interest and concern, and would be grateful for your response to the points raised below."

It then lists the items that were later published in the BuzzFeed article and concludes: "I am interested in writing a nuanced and balanced piece about the pressures of running an online news organisation in the viral internet age, and I am keen to understand the ways in which CEN helps fund your investigative journalism."

There is no reply you can make to an email like that. To my mind, it was written by an organisation that had an agenda, and that was to attack what we do. If you answer them and point out their flawed examples, they will only find more. And sure enough, disclosure, which is part of a legal case where both sides have to hand over documents relevant to the allegations, provided email traffic that revealed this was exactly what happened; every time a story proved true, it was replaced by another one believed to be fake.

Both the initial approach and the front-up letter of 4,000 words were the work of BuzzFeed's head of investigations Heidi Blake. In an email where the strategy for first contact was discussed, Alan White asks BuzzFeed UK boss Luke Lewis, BuzzFeed fake news expert Craig Silverman, the UK editorial director Tom Phillips and Heidi for their opinion, having earlier discussed the matter with Mark Schoofs, who had told him to make sure that the front up letter was sent in multiple ways.

His suggestion to reach out in as many ways as possible was later relayed to Alan White, who moved from worrying about getting beaten up by me to worrying that alarm bells might go off at the Mirror or MailOnline when they were tipped off about what BuzzFeed planned, and might then start desperately trying to scrub or change CEN copy once the BuzzFeed 'bombshell' dropped. As it turned out, not a single article was altered or removed from any Fleet Street titles, such was the influence of the BuzzFeed story on their media rivals.

But as the BuzzFeed efforts to get me to point out any errors in their story intensified, it made life hard for me, my team, and even those who knew me. A journalist ex-girlfriend in France was contacted and quizzed about our 'great work' before slamming the phone down on them when the conversation changed to what they really wanted, which was evidence of my news fakery. She called me in tears to tell me how BuzzFeed had suddenly become aggressive and demanded the truth about my agency, after first telling her honeyed words to get her to talk, of course.

Far worse than that, though, was the repetition of their cut-and-pasted narrative to my clients. To comment on what was alleged, these clients needed to be told what was claimed, and the moment that was handed over, whether BuzzFeed decided to publish the story or not, it made little difference to the damage caused in asking the question. The damage from any negative reporting on an organisation or individual is always in the way it affects those closest to the allegations, and therefore, the real harm often comes when the reporter makes the call to check the story with connected individuals or organisations. Alan White, who in his email correspondence had made it quite clear he was well aware of the agency's other more positive achievements, did not seem interested in mentioning those positive points when questioning our clients, who were also, by chance, BuzzFeed's biggest rivals in the UK market.

As Sir Arnold Wesker notes in one of my favourite books, 'Journey Into Journalism': "The journalist claims and exercises the moral right to expose other individuals whose moral righteousness they suspect." Therefore, what Alan White was doing was, on the face of it, entirely justified, but could that moral high ground still be claimed for such damaging questions when there was a considerable commercial advantage to be claimed at the same time, and more so when it was simply to repeat rumours lifted from the internet?

With the vast number of potential stories that could have been covered from things happening worldwide, and with very few investigative organisations taking on this challenge, would it not have been better to choose a target where there was not a strong commercial interest in doing so? Probably, he did not care because morally questionable though it may be, it was unlikely that any fallout would happen at the stage of fronting up because when it comes to potential libel (printed falsehoods) and slander (spoken falsehoods), a private individual can be taken to court (if the other has the money). But if you have a press card, it is an instant get-out-of-jail-free card in most jurisdictions that allows you to say or write anything to anyone as long as it is phrased as a question.

It does not matter whether that is to ask a person's employer if there is truth to the rumours they are a child molester, a tax dodger, having an affair or even, horror of horrors, the King of Bullsh*t News. With a press card, it is possible to put this sort of material to anyone, regardless of the consequences for those under the spotlight.

There is a good reason that this is allowed. If a journalist like Alan wants to write a story and believes he has the truth, he still has to give the other side a chance to put their side and get their opinion on whether the story is correct. That means he needs to be allowed to ask questions that might land anyone else with a libel or a slander writ. But it is also a powerful tool for anyone who wants to abuse it.

I was determined not to give them that opportunity once I realised they were not all they seemed. But that didn't make the wait for them to finally publish any easier; it was hanging like a sword of Damocles over my head, and the phone calls from their reporter, White, continued. All this didn't make it any easier with my already stressful day job. Senior editors in my business who knew about it, like myself, were distracted. We knew they were close to running something when BuzzFeed moved to the "front up letter," where they stopped the fake praise and put down detailed allegations before publication.

Yet still they did not publish because, incredible though it may seem, when it came to the eve of their planned publication, they were left with the unpleasant realisation that they had nothing original other than material cut and pasted from the internet. They could not go forward.

My refusal to respond to this, however, did not change the fact that they were continuing to disrupt my business; what I needed was to take control of the situation and make sure what was published was on my terms. That meant when they weren't ready and at the worst possible time for it to appear. That time was Friday evening when everybody was going home and planning the weekend.

To implement that plan, I contacted the Press Gazette. I asked them if they would be interested in a story about the fact that BuzzFeed appeared to be doing a critical story about a direct rival in the viral news business. Press Gazette told me they would look at it, if I was prepared to provide emails as proof. I agreed and made the one condition which I could, which was that it was embargoed for publication until Friday, although I didn't say why. It was and still is pretty standard for embargoes to be requested on information supplied to the media. These are done for many different reasons, and they are mostly understood and respected as a condition of being given the story.

It was a risk for me, as obviously I was unable to dictate what Press Gazette would write, and it was entirely possible that they might decide the story was not about the BuzzFeed conflict of interest but, instead, about the BuzzFeed allegations.

However, they decided that the commercial rival angle was more interesting, contacted BuzzFeed UK for a comment, and the article ran as I had hoped on a Friday afternoon.

But waiting so long and allowing me to cast doubt on their story before it was published was not BuzzFeed's only mistake. My friend Patrick Masters, the financial expert at the Sunday Times Insight team, would often be asked by editors as he pored through documents and accounts when the story he was on would be ready. His answer was always the same: the story is ready when it's ready. Nothing else should dictate publication.

BuzzFeed did not see it that way in their bid to negate the Press Gazette story as they tried to win journalistic credibility in the UK by exposing a major supplier to their rivals as a fake news factory. They were horrified when they realised the tables had been turned and it appeared they would end up in the spotlight themselves, accused of using journalism for commercial advantage.

As soon as the article[2] appeared in the Press Gazette, panic engulfed BuzzFeed. Someone had shot their fox, and within a few hours, the story they had been dithering about for months was rushed into production. They had not finished the article, and they admitted they were not ready to publish, but there was no way the egos of Luke Lewis and Ben Smith could not react, even though, with hindsight, that would have been the best thing to do.

They had also not considered that I had taken a real gamble with my story, as it was also the worst time for me to make my claims. With people only thinking about heading off for the weekend, the BuzzFeed team could probably have ignored it. But I had taken the gamble, and it had paid off.

And so on 24th April 2015, [3] after the Press Gazette request for comment, BuzzFeed's vice president of communications, Liz Wasden, their UK director, Luke Lewis, and PR supremo Alice Suh confirmed they were about to do exactly what I was hoping when I leaked the story to Press Gazette, which meant rushing to get their version of the story out there. In an email

---

[2] http://www.pressgazette.co.uk/*BuzzFeed*-investigation-emails-harm-business-competitor-online-news-provider
[3] *BuzzFeed*_009322 (Subject: *'Central European News'* – LUKE LEWIS,)

chat, Liz advises Luke not to comment and urges a speedy publication of their own version, saying in response to Press Gazette's request for comment: "Is there a chance we can publish ahead of them?" Alice has also asked the same question already, and it is she and not Luke that replies to Liz, saying: "I asked Luke about this too, but he said they aren't ready to publish it yet. Right, Luke?"

For his part, Lewis was consulting lawyers of his own, and disclosure reveals that he had written to high-profile UK media lawyer Mark Stephens in a heavily redacted document, copying in the investigation's editor Heidi Blake and BuzzFeed's assistant general counsel Nabiya Syed to try and find out what to do about the Press Gazette article. Although, as I say, heavily redacted, which means blacked out, it has that unmistakable smell of blind panic. Stephens, for his part, was able to respond quickly, as he was already well briefed: He was, after all, the one who had been dealing with the legal read of the King story and had confirmed it was good to go. If that's correct, it seems he missed a few things, or maybe BuzzFeed hadn't told him that their entire story had been hoovered up from the internet.

It was a shame for BuzzFeed, but good for me, that Heidi did not bring the Sunday Times wisdom with her when she moved to her new job: reminding her team that the story is finished when the story is finished, and nothing else should control that. Ignoring this rule when she got to BuzzFeed made my job that much easier for a legal challenge because so much of what they wrote was completely wrong. And even though superficially their story was incredibly damning, and it would be difficult to think of a harsher headline to describe any journalist, the Friday publication diffused it enough that by Monday morning, it was already old news, and that helped us to maintain our core client database, that and the fact, of course, that it wasn't true.

The strategy to force BuzzFeed's rushed publication had another advantage. It ensured that there was no take up among anyone that mattered or that my clients cared about, like Private Eye or the Media Guardian, despite BuzzFeed's best efforts. It had also failed to be the social media sensation they had hoped. And although it was admittedly widely repeated in foreign language media, even then, it was mostly only done so by the local left-wing media that wanted to attack their conservative rivals. But in the UK, where it counted and had been intended to catapult BuzzFeed to the top of the news food chain by demolishing their rivals, the story had fallen flat, and there was not a single repetition. Damp squib doesn't even come close.

So, the first major BuzzFeed UK investigation, to their amazement, merited not a word where it mattered, and even better, I had a promise from the media bible Press Gazette that if I could comprehensively refute the allegations, they would run a further story.

That support started our pushback, where we carried on against all odds, to the fury and bewilderment of the BuzzFeed editorial team. I later discovered that, even within BuzzFeed, there was still strong demand for my 'Bullsh*t News'.

Post-publication, BuzzFeed regional director for America, Conz Preti, emailed BuzzFeed's LGBT editorial team. That email had the subject: "Transgender woman stripped, shaved and pulverised by police sparking outrage, MailOnline." It was sent on the 24th of April 2015 at 7:39 pm, several hours after BuzzFeed's story about me was published.

In it, Conz wrote: "Everyone's talking about this, maybe not worth covering right now, but wanted to flag". Conz then links to the MailOnline article. One of the reporters, Nicolas Mora, then replies: "So the pics come from CEN, which we just totally debunked and disavowed as a source. Just FYI." [4]

* * *

---

[4] *BuzzFeed*_009427 (Subject: 'Transgender woman stripped, shaved and 'pulverised' by police sparking outrage / Daily Mail Online' - NONE)

CHAPTER FOUR - SECRET AGENTS

Trade Craft

Central European News, or CEN as it was known to London's Fleet Street, was and still is one of the must-check, first-call foreign news agencies that news and foreign news desks relied on. CEN had a very simple formula: we sold viral tabloid stories to earn money to fund investigations, books and documentaries.

We operated in the shadows, the general public didn't even know we were there unless they checked the picture credits closely, and this was a significant problem when BuzzFeed came to research us because while we were connected with a vast media network of publishers, the lack of bylines and agency credits made it hard to know the true extent of our network.

As they wrote in their story: "The firm's business model . . . is to sell a regular stream of stories and pictures to other media companies, which publish them under the bylines of their own reporters." And BuzzFeed went on: "They also appeal because they are perfectly tailored to the current media ecosystem, in which the holy grail is to have content go viral on Facebook and other social media platforms, delivering a surge of traffic."

I am convinced that before they moved to the UK in 2013, BuzzFeed had no idea there was a flourishing network of local agencies all over the UK providing a constant stream of material to the British media.

At least back then, many agencies like mine had no clear online presence. In most cases, we worked B2B where we were known by the people who needed to know, supplying news and information to professional media outlets directly. In more detail, these agencies grew out of the Fleet Street tradition to have stringers – a sort of local correspondent – in every major town in the United Kingdom without staff journalists already in place. As a result, agencies or freelancers like those in NAPA became the backbone of the British newspaper industry. As my friend, the late Dennis Cassidy, who ran the Cassidy & Leigh Agency, used to say, news agencies are working at the coalface of democracy. They dig, find the news nuggets, and polish them up to be displayed in newspapers and magazines, not just in the UK, but worldwide.

I don't know if anyone has ever made a proper history of these businesses, partly because most people outside the UK media scene don't even know about them, but in a nutshell, ever since editorial teams have been shrinking and withdrawing from the regions to the big cosmopolitan centres, journalists who refused to up stakes and move, and instead remained behind, still needed to work. And many decided to cover the same local patch, but this time as stringers, who are freelance.

Some of these freelancers were better than others, so they took on people to cover the workload, and if there were enough of them, they might have taken on photographers. Some of those agencies expanded to become organisations in the UK with editorial teams to rival the national newspapers they were supplying, while others have expanded far beyond the borders of the UK to become truly international news organisations.

If there was more than one agency in a patch or too little mainstream news, some might specialise. For example, an agency in Windsor specialised in the Royal family, in Manchester and Liverpool, they turned their focus to football. How each agency shaped itself was dictated by where they were located and where they believed they could get sales.

Many of these agencies are members of NAPA, where membership provides recognition and ensures other advantages, like access to press cards for agency journalists. Once a year, there was the annual awards dinner, which is about the only opportunity agency staff have to be recognised for their hard work. Our business is not selling adverts or doing high-profile PR campaigns disguised as news like BuzzFeed. It is purely about providing content to our clients.

Before BuzzFeed pigeonholed me as a viral content creator, it was enormously liberating to write about whatever I thought was interesting as a journalist. Agencies have a reputation for working staff hard, but are an important stepping-stone for young journalists to national newspapers. A few years at a news agency covering courts and councils or feature writing for magazines should almost guarantee a job at a national newspaper.

There is also the enormous influence you can have on the back of stories published worldwide, which is balanced alongside the almost zero recognition either for the agency or individual reporters. That's because, yes, the stories we create change the world, yet we rarely get the byline or agency recognition. The business works whereby we are paid for what we deliver, and recognition is not part of the deal.

BuzzFeed never followed up on its observation that my business model was to sell content to partners "which publish them under the bylines of their own reporters." But the reason was no secret. Online coverage of the annual NAPA awards by Dominic Ponsford and his team from Press Gazette was frequently focused on the fact that many of the prize winners won awards for stories that did not have their names.

In 2013, the Press Gazette's columnist named 'Axegrinder' wrote: "It's been pointed out to me that some online national newspaper journalists are garnering suspiciously high story counts. Take two online journalists from The Independent, who I won't name to save their blushes. A source tells me: 'They have the highest story counts on the staff by a long way. They are, however, two online guys, and have never reported for the Indy in their lives. They are simply instructed to put their names at the top of a lot of wire copy, so it looks better for the paper'." [5]

Move forward ten years, and not much has changed, with the notable exception of newspapers from the UK publishing group Reach, particularly the Mirror, which frequently bylines the original reporter.

In my memo to my lawyer, I offered a brief overview of my agency and the journalism we had been doing since we were founded in 1995, 20 years before the BuzzFeed story was published, to give him some idea as to why making independent media sustainable was important.

---

[5] https://pressgazette.co.uk/publishers/nationals/byline-bandits-at-the-independent-accused-of-taking-credit-for-agency-copy/

It was not about fame; if it had been, I would have gone back to the UK to be in the spotlight to attend the Paul Foot Award ceremony, which a series of stories we did about the trafficking of women had won. It was also never about the money, even though vast sums could be made. The most I was ever offered to 'support' an investigation was $500,000 to support my legal case against *BuzzFeed*, but Harry and I turned it down because we didn't think we needed it, and certainly didn't want to end up with the victory we expected to get to be tainted like the Hulk Hogan victory against Gawker that a billionaire funded. As any journalist who has gone to any press event offering refreshments knows, there is no such thing as a free drink. You always pay somewhere along the line.

What motivated me was journalism's enormous ability to make a difference, and the responsibility to use it honestly. It should never be used to try and push an agenda, only to tell the truth and put both sides in an often uneven battle to level the playing field. That sort of influence, with access to the front pages of papers like the Times or the Telegraph, where simply telling the truth could change a government or make the people we wrote about millionaires overnight, would take another book to describe. But while I shared in the joy of those to whom I gave a voice, I had always been safely on the side of doing the reporting, and I had rarely experienced what it was like to be under the media spotlight myself. The only exception was a seven-month investigation into corruption involving Austria's biggest bank and US pyramid scheme fraudster Bernie Madoff. On the eve of the book's publication, with a new family to care for, I suddenly realised that we could lose everything if the bank wanted to make life difficult. It was one of the most challenging 24 hours of my life. But then the country's largest newspaper waded in, running a series of articles backing up my allegations, and I knew we were in the clear.

But what was unique about the BuzzFeed story is that for the first time, I was the villain of the story, ruining lives and selling fake news to fund my corrupt global media empire. I wouldn't wish being stripped of a reputation that took a lifetime to build on anyone, but I have to admit that it brought home to me more than anything how important it was to have someone prepared to listen, and give a voice to the underdog.

CEN had not avoided criticism because of a shadowy network of greedy publishers covering up our dark deeds, as BuzzFeed claimed, but because the news we sent them never caused a problem. Our publishers' ability to exist rested on their credibility; they would never have risked it for a clickbait headline, and they didn't need to, as they still had large reporting teams that could deliver real news. They did not need tricks. In this equation, CEN provided reliable content year in and year out, never got them sued, and our news was always backed up with proof when someone unhappy wanted to cause a problem and complain. Having a link to a social media post, or a discredited clickbait site is not for us proof that the story is correct, despite the BuzzFeed claims to the contrary. None of these were primary sources for our material. If you want to know why no one had called us out for news fakery before, look no further than the fact that we were not doing anything to garner criticism. It was as simple as that.

But we had an Achilles heel, one that I only realised in the wake of the BuzzFeed allegations. As mentioned above, it lay in the fact that one of things we were most proud of was being able to provide a voice to those who had none, by giving them a platform to tell their stories using the most powerful media in the world. No matter how one-sided the battle, this always levelled the playing field.

Yet our weakness was that when I needed that for myself, apart from the Press Gazette, there was, at least before the court case, no one who was interested in telling our story. It was frustrating that nobody could see the contradiction in the fact that, over the decades during which we had created hundreds of thousands of news stories for sale to the biggest media brands in the world, nobody other than BuzzFeed had noticed we were apparently running a fake news factory.

So nobody else other than a rival. A rival that had an enormous commercial stake in making sure the allegations were believed. It was even more frustrating that TV, radio, newspapers and magazines around the world that ran my news had chosen not to defend it.

It was beyond ludicrous, and yet ...

It took me six weeks to examine all the many BuzzFeed claims, and by the time my 125-page rebuttal was ready, the BuzzFeed allegations had gone too far for it to make any difference.

When I'd finally been able to expose the story for what it was, and highlight the complete lack of substance, no one was interested any more.

The media had moved on and it was old news, and no longer interesting.

All anyone remembered, if they thought about it at all, was that BuzzFeed had ripped back the curtain exposing me to the world. I was the Wizard of Oz, the man who was not what he seemed. And we were definitely a million miles from Kansas.

* * *

The End of the Beginning

When the report was published, the headline was so damning that despite the fact I had expected it, the sheer length under such a headline as The King of Bullsh*t News left me in no doubt that there was no point in going on.

I closed my company, told the staff not to work, and cancelled my 50th birthday plans. Instead, I was left wondering if, being 50, I could get a job at the McDonald's down the road to try to pay my mortgage. It was the journalistic equivalent of disappearing into the study with a revolver and a stiff glass of whisky to do the decent thing.

Yet something remarkable happened as I sat in my office on the first non-working work day, a Monday, as I was alone with my thoughts.

The phone rang.

Okay, the phone ringing isn't that remarkable, but the voice at the other end was. It was one of our clients. They had not received any stories. They wanted to check whether the CEN wire service was down. I asked if they'd seen the BuzzFeed story. "Yeah", they replied, "we saw it, so what? It's only BuzzFeed". They wanted our stories, and again, they asked where they were.

More calls followed, enough of them to convince me to turn the feed back on. Even rival NAPA agencies called in to say that they would not be supplying BuzzFeed with content in the future in support of a respected colleague. They knew it was impossible to have been what BuzzFeed alleged and not be called out before. NAPA offers a complaints and reconciliation service. I was never complained about.

It might have been a different story if any media that mattered had given the BuzzFeed report credibility by republishing the allegations. But that never happened either, especially as most were probably enjoying their weekends, and The King of Bullsh*t News was old news by Monday when most were back at work. My rushing them into a Friday publication had done the trick. It was then time to start the pushback.

I started investigating the claims straight away, believing that when I showed BuzzFeed that most of the story was, as they would call it, "bullsh*t", it would have to be pulled. I had no idea it was the beginning of what would later become a legal battle that would go all the way to the US Second Circuit. That court case in New York was later to be ruled out on a pre-trial summary judgment motion.

When we appealed, BuzzFeed produced an article in the Guardian claiming that we were continuing to run a fake news factory.

It seemed irrelevant to the court that this article had been written by a former BuzzFeed staffer who had been involved in the 'King' story, and had then moved to the Guardian. He'd made no declaration of interest when repeating the 2015 allegations I ran a fake news factory on the eve of my final court showdown with BuzzFeed.

An independent outsider could have gained the distinct impression that this had been arranged precisely to trigger what BuzzFeed needed, with me and the court swept along as dupes. And so, the trial never happened, but in a sense, it was no longer important.

It was still a big win, providing me with answers in intimate detail on how BuzzFeed worked. It offered answers that helped to explain what financial titans like BuzzFeed were doing, poking around in the affairs of a media minnow like me?

* * *

CHAPTER FIVE - FACECROOKS

Anti Social

I had never wanted to go to court, and I detailed in my lawyer's report the lengths I went to for an amicable solution involving no money; all I had asked was that the story be taken down.

But I had reckoned without the determination of Ben Smith and BuzzFeed UK to see me closed down, and Luke Lewis and his team kept up its pressure for me to close, and to stop my clients using my news content. But I was pushing back. That started with six weeks of clinically taking apart the allegations and pointing out all the errors in the work.

And then I learned Luke Lewis was to be replaced.

I don't doubt that he was moved aside seemingly in a rush after the story not only flopped, but was found to be so badly flawed that it even resulted in a Parliamentary question in Austria where my agency is based. His swift removal was underlined by the fact that his replacement Janine Gibson's introduction to the job seems to have been brought forward before she was ready.

When Gibson was contacted after the announcement about her new role, and was asked if she would be making a statement about the CEN issue, she said she was still in the US on a fact-finding tour, and was not yet taking up the role for which she had been hired.

In the appointment of the former Guardian journalist and editor Gibson, I saw a glimmer of hope for a resolution. I felt almost certain that with her Guardian background, she would be sure to put things right when I reached out to her.

In researching her, I was also pleased to be reminded that I had worked for her on the specialist publication Broadcast. She was the international editor between 1987 and 1998, when I was appointed as their Central European Correspondent.

In addition, the Media Guardian had been a regular client. We had worked for the site's editor Lisa O'Carroll, and more significantly, we had then worked for her successor, Steve Busfield, to whom we regularly pitched stories. I am pretty sure he would have given me a good reference, especially as, by a weird coincidence, it turned out he was married to Janine Gibson.

When she got my letter, she ignored it, but then again, that may have been because she was too busy copying BuzzFeed's strategy of using editorial to attack rivals, especially when she had a grudge.

After leaving the Guardian to take up her BuzzFeed job, she didn't waste much time in getting a team to produce what Private Eye described as an "epically dull 5,313 word screed on 'How the Guardian Lost America'" although the article [6] was at pains to say she was 'not' involved in its production, she was the editor-in-chief.

---

[6] https://www.*BuzzFeed*.com/stevenperlberg/how-the-guardian-lost-america?utm_term=.se9Q4dVap#.qmVOqDPW4

Not involved?

Really?

It detailed at length how the Guardian's US operations had gone pear-shaped in recent times – notably in the "years after winning a Pulitzer Prize for the Edward Snowden story". That means, of course, the years after Janine Gibson and HER Edward Snowden story. The BuzzFeed article was written by Stephen Perlberg, a reporter based in BuzzFeed's office in Manhattan, a train ride from the outpost in Brooklyn where the Guardian produced its own online offering. In addition to this obvious rivalry, as Private Eye noted, "BuzzFeed's UK editor-in-chief is Janine Gibson, who used to be in charge of the Guardian's US operation up to the point when it, err, won a Pulitzer for the Edward Snowden story."

The magazine noted that Gibson subsequently left the Guardian 'in high dudgeon' after failing to succeed Alan Rusbridger as editor in 2015. Katharine Viner, who got the job, was castigated in Perlberg's piece for her "overspending and missed opportunities" during her own period in charge of the US operation.

Perlberg noted that both Viner and Gibson "declined to comment for this story" which started with the opening paragraph: "The Guardian's US newsroom didn't become the voice of the Bernie left during the election. It didn't break huge campaign scoops. Years after winning a Pulitzer for the Edward Snowden story, Guardian US has slashed costs, leaving employees stewing about mismanagement, infighting, a sexual harassment allegation, and unrealistic business expectations."

So CEN had complained about the vested interest journalism of her new team, and not only had she ignored it, but she ended up being implicated in doing exactly the same thing herself. As the old adage goes, "if you can't beat them, join them."

It was a rude introduction to how powerless one can be on the other side of negative media coverage. One that underlined exactly why our provision of coverage to people who would otherwise struggle to be heard when taking on a powerful rival had been so well received by those we focused on. I had tried everything to avoid court, but nothing had worked. In the UK, complaints about inaccurate reporting can be swiftly dealt with by what used to be the Press Complaints Commission (PCC), which was later replaced by the Independent Press Standards Organisation (IPSO).

But BuzzFeed was never a member of either, and as a result, the only way to get a retraction or correction was to appeal to them, and if that did not work, to take them to court. That or ignore it, but to ignore injustice was not in my nature. I had fought enough for others. Now, when there was no one else, it was time to do it for myself.

I had started my battle against BuzzFeed believing that you couldn't cut and paste material to create a 6,958-word article about a commercial rival with a clear vested interest without consequences. From Private Eye to IPSO, there was always a way of at least highlighting this vested interest. Legal action was seemingly the last option, yet through all the many hearings, they got away with it right the way to the US Supreme Court.

The biggest problem, of course, was and still is that few in my profession of journalism have the time to look beyond the surface or to write anything that is not handed to them on a plate, and in a sense, I was lucky that for whatever reason the Press Gazette had taken a largely sympathetic attitude to our position, that and the fact that none of the clients had marked us as a problem agency, despite BuzzFeed's claim our news fakery was an 'open secret'.

Regarding the rest of the media, which mostly ignored our story beyond extensively reporting the court case as it rumbled on, I don't blame them for that. Despite the campaigning reporting we had once done, funded by viral consent, we had also been starting to experience the same problem of paying for it even before the BuzzFeed story. The amount of campaigning investigative reporting we were producing, content that my accounts team called 'charity journalism' because it never covered its costs, had already been dwindling to the point where unless I was paid for the investigation by a media partner, I mostly didn't have the time to do it. A single investigation typically takes around three days solid at the very least, often spread piecemeal over a more extended period. In contrast, a national newspaper reporter who applied for a job here revealed that he had a quota of six stories daily in London. There was little original reporting; instead, he typically needed to rewrite a report from another publication, come up with the headline, lay it out on the page with pictures and videos when available, provide captions, and promote it on social media afterwards.

It's no wonder that there was little coverage of my case beyond what was happening at each stage of the court case. Yet despite the lack of focus on the other things we were doing, as the hard-fought battle with BuzzFeed continued, the ordeal also defined my new project for the future, NewsX.

Essentially, the NewsX concept involves filling the areas described as "news deserts", which are gaps left in the media landscape by the closure of local newspapers and specialist magazines, with small news agencies.

Like the lost media they will replace, these NewsX communities produce news, but unlike them, they have no advertising and cannot easily be corrupted. In fact, quite the opposite, because they rely on independence and credibility for their existence. This credibility is the one thing they need to ensure material is published by our real press media partners, who validate NewsX community content with the stamp of their own brands.

These NewsX communities will be set up inside social media groups and put the information they provide through the filter of journalism, feeding what is approved by editors into a global network where a sophisticated taxonomy matches editorial communities with publishers.

Without the vast distribution costs and the extensive infrastructure of the legacy media they work for, these communities become far more economically viable, making them not only sustainable, but also scalable.

This solution has taken more than two decades to evolve, constantly reinventing itself to match the challenges. It was ultimately forged by the strategies we applied to our newsroom which helped us survive the attack by BuzzFeed, a rival with almost 2000 staff around the world and at one time valued at $1.7 billion.

We survived, but not without cost, of which one of the most painful was the fact that so many stories landed on my desk that would have been so much more worthwhile than this one. But I did not choose the story, it chose me: That was laid down when BuzzFeed journalist Alan White wrote an email with the subject 'No Surprises Letter' to his BuzzFeed colleagues. In his email, he noted: "We're about to destroy a business that took him over a decade to build along with his entire professional credibility." [7]

That statement was not even half of it, as it also cost my funding for things like my Fourth Estate Project, which never got off the ground but was later to be reinvented as NewsX, and the closure of my online news sites or fringe projects like managing Kim Petras, a German singer. A lawyer in New York with whom I had developed a friendship while working on a financial fraud investigation never spoke to me again when I asked if she had seen the article. She had initially sympathised with me before she knew the details, she told me she would have a look at it and would maybe offer some advice, but after doing just that, and reviewing the BuzzFeed allegations, she never spoke to me again. These and others were all hard things to swallow.

My Sunday Times Insight friend Patrick Masters summed it up perfectly when I complained no one would listen to my side of the story, and could not see that BuzzFeed were the real 'Kings of Bullsh*t News'. He told me, quite correctly: "But you would say that, wouldn't you."

I had to admit he had a point. If I was on the other side, I doubt I would have listened to me either. As I say, the other journalists who could and should have listened were, like me before April 2015, probably too busy with other things.

Another person who helped put things into perspective and warned me that there are many reasons to avoid going to court was my lawyer, Harry Wise, whom I met through a producer from ABC Nightline when we worked on our exclusive story about Dr Heinrich Gross, the Nazi medic who experimented on and murdered children considered "unclean" by the Nazi regime under its Euthanasia Program. I reached out to Harry because a New York magazine had been taking content and not paying for it, and I decided that although I would probably end up paying more than I earned, it would be best to get a lawyer to chase down the payment. That lawyer was Harry, and it turned out that the magazine was just down the road from his office. He went down there during his lunch hour and handed them the bill, which they then paid the same day. He said he didn't often get the chance to do that in person, and the look of surprise on the face of the editor when a lawyer turned up with a bill had been worth it. As it was no more than a couple of hours of work, he never charged me, and it was like that as we continued to discuss various legal matters over the years where there was never a charge, even though it was probably many hours altogether.

So, I trusted Harry, and there was no question that I would use him if we decided to pursue this in court. BuzzFeed had its office in New York, and he was a New York lawyer, so it was a logical fit. Before going to court, Harry counselled me with the words of New York judge Learned Hand, who said: "I must say that as a litigant, I should dread a lawsuit beyond almost anything else short of sickness and death." I now know the truth of those words, and with their powerful legal muscle, BuzzFeed buried us in legal complications.

---

[7] *BuzzFeed_010286* (Subject: 'No surprises letter' – ALAN WHITE, LUKE LEWIS, TOM PHILLIPS, CRAIG SILVERMAN, HEIDI BLAKE,) *

But back then, after much indecision and talking it over with my wife, we were happy to proceed. It was announced to the world in January 2016, getting widespread coverage in many places, including Press Gazette.[8] But despite Harry's warning, I had greatly underestimated the stress of the process.

Disclosure alone allows your opponents to crawl over every aspect of your life. Of course, it works both ways, but whereas we handed over everything and withheld nothing apart from one redacted name in one document, BuzzFeed kept back hundreds of documents and hid sections in hundreds more by blacking them out. What they did hand over was produced in such bad quality that it was impossible to search properly for keywords, so documents needed to be scoured by hand, which was weeks of work every time we did it.

The table listing the redacted material where they hid details under pages of black ink runs to over 100 pages, with dozens of documents on every page, and there are another 68 pages of documents that were not handed over at all for reasons that include attorney-client privilege. In contrast, BuzzFeed demanded disclosure of every aspect of CEN's business,[9] whereas CEN only asked for details of anything relevant to the production of the article. Their demands were a double burden because, as a journalist, you also have the duty of confidentiality to those you have worked with.

When the first batch of thousands of documents turned up from BuzzFeed's lawyers, produced in such bad quality that it was impossible to properly search the PDFs, and everything needed to be read, I had no energy left. What turned things around was when Patrick Masters, who before he was at the Sunday Times was a Wall Street and later City of London trader, offered to do the job for me. The gems he found in that first batch answered some of my many questions and, more importantly, removed the "writer's block" I had about tackling it myself.

Yet in doing so, despite finding more evidence as to motivation and piecing together how it all came together, it was doing this that made the litigation almost a sideshow, something that I should have seen long ago. The profession had been diluted by those who do not share the real values of journalism, and work for so many other masters to the point where it faces a credibility crisis. I knew social media giants like Facebook took our content and used it to claim our advertising. But what I found on this journey shows that other organisations themselves, of which BuzzFeed was the first and worst offender, had set about destroying what was left of the media landscape from the inside. They did that by dismantling valued traditions that were there for a reason, such as the need to have clear separation between advertising and editorial.

What happened to CEN was another example of what BuzzFeed had been doing all the time. While other publishers may have tainted their reputations with paid content, BuzzFeed took this to a whole new level, attacking rivals and boosting their commercial interests and those of their partners through their content. As I found out from Ben Smith's book 'Traffic', this included informing on the tricks of their rivals. BuzzFeed, for example, had discussed a

---

[8] https://pressgazette.co.uk/media_law/news-agency-boss-sues-*BuzzFeed*-11m-over-king-bullsh*t-news-slur/
[9] https://pressgazette.co.uk/publishers/digital-journalism/*BuzzFeed*-accused-of-fishing-expedition-over-request-to-see-ten-years-of-emails-from-news-agency-suing-it-for-11m/

partnership with a company called Upworthy. It was founded in March 2012 by the former executive director of the leading US online political organisation MoveOn, Eli Pariser, as well as Peter Koechley, the former managing editor of The Onion. The pair had proved to be much more talented than BuzzFeed at harnessing Facebook's growing powers.

Smith revealed how Eli had started with MoveOn.org at the age of 23, leading its controversial protests against the Iraq War. In 2008, Eli used MoveOn's massive email list largely in service of electing Barack Obama. Smith said: "Eli was among the first to see what was changing. While I watched Twitter suck the energy and audience out of my blog at Politico, Eli was looking at Facebook, which was on a trajectory, even by 2011, to dwarf the rest of the internet."

After the 2008 election, Eli wrote a book called 'The Filter Bubble', in which he warned that the subtle personalisation pioneered by Facebook and other platforms would "serve up a kind of invisible autopropaganda, indoctrinating us with our own ideas, amplifying our desire for things that are familiar and leaving us oblivious to the dangers lurking in the dark territory of the unknown."

His new creation, Upworthy, was on the up from the start, receiving nine million views by the middle of 2012, an astonishing start, the sort of traffic numbers people worked years for. The formula was simple: a YouTube video embedded on a page, and a headline to make you click: "Bully Calls News Anchor Fat, News Anchor Destroys Him on Live TV" drew more than four million views. "Mitt Romney Accidentally Confronts a Gay Veteran; Awesomeness Ensues" got nearly three million.

Smith noted that Fast Company called Upworthy "a soulful BuzzFeed," adding, "it was true that there was something about its purity that made us nervous".

He said that while BuzzFeed had been trying to deliver straight news and politics mixed with the silliest and strangest parts of internet culture, Eli was unabashedly using emotion to package political content. Smith added: "It seemed to be the merger of information and emotion that Jonah had been searching for. I wondered if he regretted hiring me to produce harder news."

Smith revealed that while Upworthy seemed unstoppable, rising to a peak of eighty-seven million monthly views in November of 2013, that ended when Peretti had 'shared' information with Facebook that, by chance, also turned out to be the reason for the collapse of Upworthy's traffic.

In the same month Upworthy celebrated its November 2013 monthly views, a top Facebook 'News Feed' engineer had stopped by at BuzzFeed. Smith said: "After he left, Jonah wrote to him about what he saw as a persistent problem in Facebook's feed, the one Upworthy was particularly famous for exploiting."

It is not possible to underestimate how vital access to Facebook's 'News Feed' was for BuzzFeed. 'News Feed' was the part of Facebook that could completely make or break a publisher with an algorithm tweak, and they often did. News Feed controlled what was shared with users on the Facebook network, including profile changes, upcoming events and birthdays, and, of course, news.

After that conversation, a series of Facebook tweaks were used to decimate Upworthy traffic, encouraging users to watch videos directly on Facebook instead. One competitor less for BuzzFeed, and never mind all the news organisations that needed ad revenue from the video that presumably also got turned off by the same tweaks?

Peretti shared what he had told Facebook with Smith: "It's really fun collaborating with Facebook's team on how 'News Feed' should work."

Fun?

It was also something any other news publisher would have paid an arm and a leg for.

Upworthy's technical proficiency at maximising traffic returns was, it had turned out, also a weakness that Facebook, once it had learned about it, or been told about it, had been able to close down.

So Upworthy and CEN and BuzzFeed were all experimenting with what Smith described as straight news and politics mixed with "the silliest and strangest parts of internet culture". In hindsight, it was rather like sharing a nest with a Magpie, because as far as BuzzFeed's actions seemed to show, there was clearly only room for one.

Smith confessed: "Jonah had begun to make a habit of cultivating the mid-senior-level Facebook employees who ran its key product, 'News Feed'. He invited them by BuzzFeed's familiar-feeling offices when they were in New York, and stopped by to say hi when he was in the Bay Area. Over coffee in San Francisco, and in spontaneous direct messages on Twitter, Jonah could offer them the one thing Facebook didn't have: insight into how traffic was moving around its rival networks, Twitter and Pinterest."

According to Smith, a top Facebook executive said: "It was easier to talk to him without having to translate than it was to talk to most media executives."

He added: "They knew Jonah was pushing them, trying to persuade them to shape their service in a way that would help BuzzFeed—but it was nice to talk to someone who thought this new medium could make the world better, who saw you as an ally, not an alien."

If anyone wants to know why Facebook made such devastating decisions for the broader media landscape, as we tried to turn our readers and viewers of content into online traffic, the fact they were using Jonah Peretti for insights into how news worked is a horrifying prospect.

At BuzzFeed, its content in its many forms was only about traffic; traffic was all that counted. It had even persuaded partner sites to install programming code that allowed the company to monitor their traffic. By the time Ben Smith joined, the network had encompassed some 200 sites with 355 million users. The analytical capacity gave BuzzFeed an enormous trove of data about what information people were reading and how they were sharing it.

But Smith said it was more than just the insights this network gave that Facebook needed, adding that "unlike most in media, Peretti seemed to speak their language, without clumsy simplification from the pompous jargon of journalism."

Journalism?

Who needs that?

As an aside, if you want to know what Facebook is like without news, ask the Australians. In February 2021, Facebook wiped all of the news from its platform in protest at plans to force it to share its profits with local media outlets by the Australian government.

The New York Times' Sydney-bureau chief, Damien Cave, wrote at the time: "More frightening was what remained: pages dedicated to aliens and U.F.O.s; one for a community group called Say No to Vaccines; and plenty of conspiracy theories, some falsely linking 5G to infertility, others spreading lies about Bill Gates and the end of the world." [10]

It underlines why Peretti's investment in his relationships with Facebook paid off, at least short-term for BuzzFeed, as the social media platform slowly became the world's most important source of traffic.

Smith had also detailed how BuzzFeed had helped refine the tools it needed to replace news media, as when Facebook's media liaison person, Jason White, had called him with an exciting offer where Facebook was trying out a new formula for measuring the "sentiment" that users felt toward the candidates who were gearing up to run for the 2016 presidential election the following year.

He said: "Facebook would give it to us on a nearly exclusive basis, presumably because its PR team figured that Jonah and I were friendlier to the company and would have a better understanding of how it actually worked, than many of our rivals."

Either that, or they were too naive to realise the dangers of playing with fire.

Smith had even added: "I wasn't under any illusions about why they were offering us this valuable new stream of data. It was PR for their ad business. Facebook wanted to prove to candidates and campaigns that it was a real player in politics—that going through its platform was a better use of your money than buying television ads. Facebook wasn't just the place for spontaneous youth movements. It was a place you could practice politics, rally passions, raise money, maybe even change minds. Of course, Facebook's pitch matched our agenda, and our beliefs—that social media was the real show, not a sideshow, and that BuzzFeed was on track to replace the struggling New York Times for a new generation of readers, not just to supplement it. That didn't seem crazy. Jonah was already raising more money and beginning to talk to NBCUniversal about a round that would value the company at $1.7 billion . . ."

Smith had then obligingly announced the partnership with a fanfare:

"We at BuzzFeed News are deeply excited to have a powerful new window into the largest political conversation in America."

". . . the viral, mass conversation about politics on Facebook and other platforms has finally emerged as a third force in the core business of politics, mass persuasion."

Americans, said Smith, would be getting their news from trusted friends, not suspect, one-way, old-fashioned media.

---

[10] https://www.theatlantic.com/technology/archive/2022/07/facebook-without-news-would-be-worse/670933/

He added: "I knew I was doing Facebook's advertising sales team a solid here, and I heard later that they'd loved my essay. That was why they were sharing the data with us in the first place."

So once again, that's alright then!

Yet ironically, BuzzFeed's experimentation with getting traffic seems to have caused Facebook to switch from its cosy relationship with them after a story about 'The Dress'. The viral story centred on a photograph of a dress where everyone who saw it disagreed on whether it was blue and black or white and gold.

In an interview in Press Gazette where he reflected on the BuzzFeed of a decade ago, the clueless Luke Lewis noted: "The internet was a happier place. A lot of former BuzzFeed people, we like to talk about, 'what was the last good day on the internet?' A lot of people say that it was the dress. On that day, it was a real phenomenon. That was an example of internet culture that was wholesome and joyful. And often those really big viral moments were joyful and wholesome in a way that isn't true anymore."

Joyful if you are not the creators of the content. A small footnote to the history of the dress came when the original authors of the photograph that sparked the viral phenomenon complained over being "completely left out from the story", including their lack of control over the story, the omission of their role in the discovery, and the commercial use of the photograph. That, at least, is something that has not changed.

But it also marked the turning point in Facebook's friendly relationship with BuzzFeed, which was to see the switching off of its income stream that resulted in the closure of the UK team and, along with it, most of Lewis' BuzzFeed UK colleagues.

How did the dress cause that? Facebook executive Adam Mosseri, who was in charge of its 'News Feed', discussed it with Peretti and asked him, "How often do you think things should go viral like the dress?"

Smith revealed: "Jonah was surprised by the question—and by the idea that the frequency of things going viral was up to Mosseri's team. The conversation made clear to Jonah that Facebook was worried about something new: losing control. To them, the dress hadn't been a goofy triumph: it had been a kind of a bug, something that scared them. The dress itself was harmless, but the next meme to colonize the entire platform within minutes might not be, and this one had moved too fast for the (Facebook) team to control."

Too late, Peretti had seen the same threat of censorship as with the Chinese Communist Party, who had discovered that they could stop a social movement from starting without totally wiping it out, just by deleting some of its content, enough to prevent it from achieving escape velocity.

Facebook's solution, Smith said, wasn't to abandon its algorithms, which could predict what you'd like and show it to you; it was to tighten the scope in which those algorithms worked. From now on, he said, Facebook was determined to do a better job at keeping people in their lanes and bubbles.

He added: "We at BuzzFeed might have seen the dress as the beginning of a new kind of global culture, but in fact, nothing quite like it was ever allowed to happen again."

Too late did BuzzFeed realise this reality when their clever advertisements no longer went viral all on their own, along with other victims of their activities like the real news stories produced by legacy media. Gradually, Facebook had taken a larger and larger cut, and had instituted rules that pretty much required that publishers pay to have their clients' ads promoted on the site.

Smith said: "The prices you had to pay Facebook to send your sponsored content across the web varied with the season, but always rose around Christmas, and in late 2018, BuzzFeed suddenly found itself spending millions to distribute the branded posts and videos that had long been its main source of revenue."

By the time the books had closed on 2018, the company made more than $307 million—but spent $386 million to make it, a loss of more than $78 million.

To those who have experienced Ben Smith's way of doing journalism, the above extract is one of many that shows why his book on the era turned out to be the longest confession in history.

And despite my court case being derailed by the Guardian's former BuzzFeed reporter providing his old team with the material they needed to end my legal fight, still, the fight went on.

Despite the court refusing to let it go to trial, it allowed the almost complete picture of BuzzFeed's twisted approach to news to emerge, piece by piece, line by line, in thousands of documents and in the depositions taken under oath when my lawyer questioned BuzzFeed's witnesses in preparation for the trial.

The libel case, for example, meant that BuzzFeed had to admit that their team, including CFO Mark Frackt, were discussing me in some 150 individual documents at the start of 2014, precisely a decade ago. But their legal team had come up with arguments that allowed them to black out every single word. This process, known as redaction, is only supposed to be used to delete confidential data.

The court accepted this cover-up, yet a search of his LinkedIn page showed Frackt was responsible for BuzzFeed's "international expansion, editorial and commerce initiatives". It is not a huge stretch to believe that this particular part of his role is what led him to discuss my firm and me.

Only in May 2014 did the conversation expand to include the head of the UK team, Luke Lewis, and details of what they were discussing started to appear, such as our work for their MailOnline rivals, also the biggest online newspaper in the world. BuzzFeed wanted to be in the same place they were and, buoyed with hundreds of millions in investment, had set out to tackle their rival on their own doorstep by moving to the UK.

Smith had offered large salaries and a funky new office serving up caviar in the heart of London to lure staff from rivals like Associated Newspapers, publisher of the MailOnline. As these new recruits joined his team, he started to understand the rich tradition of news in the

UK and why the country had been the birthplace of such organisations as the BBC and numerous other globe-spanning media brands.

They also learned about NAPA and that the UK had a unique network of small, independent news agencies like mine, numbering in the hundreds and scattered across the country. These agencies worked at the frontline of gathering news, covering local courts, politics, and anything else on their doorstep.

However, unlike local papers, we did not publish what we created. Instead, we sold stories to other media. BuzzFeed's newly formed UK team found out from a story in the Press Gazette that my news agency, Central European News, was one of the biggest suppliers to their main rival, the MailOnline. And then a story was published that branded me The King of Bullsh*t News.

Coincidence?

I don't think so, but you can make up your own mind. When Frackt became involved with CEN in 2014, BuzzFeed was valued at 850 million dollars. By its peak in 2016, a year after they published their story, Comcast's NBCUniversal had invested an additional 200 million dollars in the company, valuing BuzzFeed at around 1.7 billion dollars.

To put that in context, it was about the same as the market capitalisation of the New York Times, the very top of the tree in US media publishing. At one point, I found evidence that they had tried to get a fifth columnist to work at our newsroom in Vienna, and on another, they plotted to plant fake news stories in a bizarre attempt at a sting operation that, not surprisingly, never happened.

Once it was published, BuzzFeed continued to pursue other stories about my agency and me, demanding action from our publishing partners, who were coincidentally the main BuzzFeed rivals in the UK, as to why they were still using us.

Publishing the story when it finally happened was bad enough. After all, BuzzFeed already had phenomenal traffic with their own pages, but it was not left there. I found, for example, that it was translated as well for further publication on their own sites, like the BuzzFeed site in France. BuzzFeed had also signed a deal with Duolingo,[11] the web app pioneering the use of gameplay theories to help teach its users foreign languages. In essence, the partnership allowed it to rely on unpaid students to do the work. BuzzFeed supplied their articles to Duolingo, which in turn assigned them to students to translate as part of a lesson plan. The students' work was then collated, proofed, and returned to BuzzFeed for publication.

I don't know how many languages the story was translated into, but they promoted it on social media, encouraging it to be shared and repeated worldwide. On BuzzFeed, every reporter was also a social media reporter, according to their boast. So it was posted and shared across numerous social media profiles and accounts.

On 24 April 2015, the same day the BuzzFeed story went live, the former Telegraph letters page editor, Robert Colvile, was writing to social@BuzzFeed.com saying: "Hi guys - can we

---

[11] https://www.forbes.com/sites/parmyolson/2013/11/13/language-app-duolingo-to-translate-more-sites-after-buzzfeed-and-cnn/

please promote this from UK accounts, and maybe even US if you like it?" This email is most probably a group email to members of the team dealing with the BuzzFeed social media accounts, who would be responsible for sharing and promoting content, and sure enough, he then provides a link to BuzzFeed's story about me and Central European News. [12]

He also does the same thing later when a BuzzFeed staff member called Gavon Laessig asks if there is anything that needs to be promoted that evening for the weekend, and Colvile replies by urging further promotion of the story, saying: "The CEN piece would be nice!". Anyone in the media might point out that on a big story that had been so much work, they would want to get as much kudos from the effort as possible. But I don't think many would agree with what was written the next day in an email on 25 April, 2015, a Saturday, and the same day I first read the BuzzFeed story as I was walking to my garden. Although it was the weekend, Luke Lewis had logged in to send a note to the three reporters who shared byline on the story, Alan White, Craig Silverman and Tom Phillips, as well as Robert Colvile, with the subject CEN:

". . . so, what comes next? How do we follow-up, keep up the pressure? If anyone of these publishers DOESN'T immediately stop dealing with CEN it looks terrible for them. Should we ring round on Monday?" [13]

Robert Colvile is the first reply, and the first thing he does is add Heidi into it and then suggest a list of ideas that take the BuzzFeed level of animosity towards CEN to a whole new level.

". . . there are a few things we want to do . . .
"Try to stir a wider interest, e.g., with Roy Greenslade and other media commentators.
"Find out what Press Gazette was smoking (not so urgent, this one)
"Pursue the JWB angle.
"Ask that CEN gives us the details of its internal investigation, or even do a breakout news post on that.
"Demand that it appoints an independent figure to review its output?
"Keep collecting examples as time permits.
"Check with the Mail/Mirror what their conclusion is, and whether they'll carry on using its content.
"Any other thoughts? Judging by the internal review line, trying to tough it out, so are in for the long haul . . .
Rob [14]

This is a really strong indication, if any more was needed, that they wanted to force CEN to close, and that this was personal. Why was he talking about the long haul? Journalists are not police organisations or activists. It's the job of journalism to put information out there and to shine a light on the good and the bad. However, news organisations shouldn't get personally involved in how their material is acted on if there is wrongdoing. That is why there are police, regulators, or even the court of public opinion.

---
[12] *BuzzFeed*_008375 (Subject: 'Investigation into *CEN*' – ROBERT COLVILE,)
[13] *BuzzFeed*_005723 (Subject: '*CEN*' – HEIDI BLAKE, CRAIG SILVERMAN, LUKE LEWIS, ROBERT COLVILE, TOM PHILLIPS, ALAN WHITE,) *
[14] *BuzzFeed*_002553

Most importantly, if there was evidence to justify it, it would be normal to hand the information over to the police. But beyond that, the end goal was always publication. But BuzzFeed did much more. Later still, for example, Robert Colvile wrote to Roy Greenslade on his private email address to keep up the pressure saying: "Hi Roy, we've never met, but we are publishing a BuzzFeed story that might interest you as an industry observer – it's an investigation of the site that provides much of the too-good-to-be-true content on the web . . . Am happy to talk you through if you're at all interested? My mobile is [telephone number]." [15]

Unlike Colville, I knew Roy Greenslade personally. We had met a few times, including at a NAPA dinner where we sat together, and he was interested enough to later write a story about me and my Journalism Without Borders project in his column.

But this sort of pressure seems to be part of the new media landscape, and proof, if any was needed, that what BuzzFeed was doing was no longer journalism, it was activism at best, assassination at worst. The reality of this new way of filling the news pages was underlined in a statement by Peretti when he told Adweek what he looks for in employees: "People who really understand how information is shared on Twitter and Facebook and Instagram and other emerging platforms, because that is in some cases as important as, you know, having traditional reporting talent."

This statement explains why the story about me was only the tip of the iceberg, with much more happening behind the scenes to such an extent that I am honestly amazed we are still in business today.

But then, I didn't know all this at the time I read the headline and the damning contents. I also had not seen, as I worked directly for my foreign desk contacts, that the journalism that I knew and had been so involved in for years was dying, only to be replaced by something else that had nothing to do with it.

According to Smith, this change, which I would call the beginning of the rot, started in November 2004. That was when George W. Bush won the US presidential election, and Republicans secured control of the Senate. Activism disguised as journalism gathered pace during what Smith described as Democratic 'grief and panic', when Arianna Huffington invited Kenneth Lerer to a gathering on 3 December, 2004, at her home.

Huffington was apparently keen to tackle this reverse in Democratic fortunes by building a news platform for them. Lerer made a seven-figure donation as he took up the role of the moneyman, while Huffington brought in social connections and media attention. They envisioned creating a platform that could wield significant cultural and political influence on news articles and media decisions.

They realised that the shiny new toy of the Internet was what people really wanted, providing information that helped them make decisions, and they decided to use it to supply a diet of activism and thinly disguised PR.

Because people turned to the Internet to find stuff to reinforce what they wanted to do anyway, it worked, and the only trick was getting in there first.

---

[15] *BuzzFeed*_008745 (Subject: '*BuzzFeed* story' – ROBERT COLVILE, Roy Greenslade)

They only needed to provide ready-made political views that matched what the people behind the traffic wanted to hear, or pass on messages advertisers wanted them to share to sell stuff.

Any stuff.

They didn't believe in journalism because that involved giving people all the information they needed to make a decision, and sometimes, that included things they didn't want people to know.

Lerer brought in Peretti, and he then created BuzzFeed as a side project to do the sort of news even the Huffington Post did not want, and to move over anything that worked to get traffic for the 'Post'. Lerer was a fan of Peretti's fake news stunts to bring in traffic that had started with an appearance on the US Today show after a viral thread over a pair of Nike trainers.

It taught him how to attract people's attention and gain traffic, and other stunts followed. He worked with his comedian sister on a project called Black People Love Us, and then the Rejection Hot Line, a phone number women could use to get rid of unwanted suitors in the pre-swipe-left Tinder days.

There were many others, all stunts created purely to get traffic. Like BuzzFeed, the Huffington Post represented a new type of media that was more about activism than journalism, about getting clicks regardless of how much value it gave to the visitor, and where anything goes in the relentless drive for traffic to attract revenue, then more investments, and then to expand again.

In those crazy online investment days, when people were prepared to lose millions rather than miss out on what could be the world's new big thing, it fuelled a whole spate of projects that pandered to the prejudices of investors looking to bolster at first the left, and then later the right to counter it, brokering a polarisation in society that spread from the US to the rest of the world when it was a strategy copied by social media. Those who scored the most traffic were those who gave people what they wanted to hear, news that made them feel good about themselves, and that anyone who felt different was somehow at least less worthy and possibly deranged.

What these new media challengers had been doing was not journalism, but if they'd admitted that, it would have been ignored, so bit by bit, they set about replacing journalism with activism and pretending both things were the same.

They are not. In journalism, balance is essential, but in activism, only information or facts supporting the narrative are good and shared; the rest is bad, and a story never to be told.

When BuzzFeed found out about my role in a Paul Foot Award for my agency's exposé on trafficking in women, which was the UK equivalent of a Pulitzer, they felt it was not of interest. Our exposé on the Nazi doctor who had escaped justice after experimenting on children was likewise rejected.

On the other hand, when a minor influencer suggested that a pink kitten people were claiming was dead was alive, and we had reported the claims, it was all hands on deck to weave it in to the narrative in support of the Ben Smith headline.

As BuzzFeed's activism disguised as journalism saw it go from strength to strength, Smith noted how legacy media ". . . cared who was reading, not how many. They measured themselves by the old standards of journalism: power, relevance, impact."

Legacy media realised too late that every visit to a clickbait site was a click that they were no longer getting, and slowly, they were sidelined and withered away as funding faded. In front of their eyes, vast and now mostly discredited media empires were created like BuzzFeed or the Huffington Post or Gawker, competing amongst themselves for traffic, and ultimately, both newcomers and traditional legacy news media lost out when the social media giants decided to grab it all for themselves.

But before that happened, it was the day of BuzzFeed, the Huffington Post, and others that had emerged as something new. Yet despite their promises of a new world order, they were only about financial reward, promoting their own interests, and activism in the disguise of journalism in favour of an owner's pet project or the writer's political affiliations.

But activism, advertising, and financial reward (beyond a fair wage) have no place in journalism. As I found out, BuzzFeed, in particular, was the originator of an even more damaging trend that arguably did more damage than anything else: tearing down the wall between advertising and editorial so that no one could tell the difference anymore. They even allowed vested interests free access to their editorial pages, if the price was right.

Tragically, as legacy media rivals struggled to meet rising costs, they embraced the same dual strategy of paid content disguised as editorial, giving followers what they wanted to hear to keep them coming back rather than what they needed to hear. Unable to beat BuzzFeed and its like, they decided to join them, and the media landscape marched on oblivious and Lemming-like to the cliff edge.

In the battle for clicks that the new media like BuzzFeed and the Huffington Post ultimately lost, not only did they destroy the media landscape, but they also hoovered up millions in investment so that they could play at a twisted form of journalism. This robbed the real media with tradition and respect for such soon-to-be-outdated concepts as the separation between church and state of funding that would have fuelled their own transformations.

* * *

CHAPTER SIX - MAIL ORDER

Post Mortem Slackers

One of the recurring themes during my research concerned the possible motivation behind the BuzzFeed story, which cost tens of thousands to produce and then a seven-figure sum to defend.

One of the sources I had hoped would yield more was the online chat forum Slack, after I found that BuzzFeed used it extensively. However, only two conversations were provided for this legal case. I tried to point out that this absence of Slack material seemed suspicious, especially in the wake of the statement by one former BuzzFeed news journalist who told Press Gazette: "It (BuzzFeed) had a big Slack culture. People talked on Slack a lot, made lots of jokes. People spent lots of time on Twitter making jokes – there were lots of big personalities on Twitter. So it meant that sometimes, the office was really quiet."

Another source said: "The newsroom was completely silent because we did everything on Slack. Talking was frowned upon." Yet although I was given thousands of emails, they claimed to have only two Slack conversations that were, admittedly, on their own damning enough, but still. . .

One was a mutual back-slapping session with lots of bonding over what one of the participants describes as "so much hate for CEN. Noted!". It seems the use of the word 'f*ck' was obligatory. Instead of treating their responsibility to do a proper job on a story that they knew was going to have 'terrible' consequences for me and my agency, they simply discussed cutting and pasting, interspersed with statements like "F*cking CEN", "I hate CEN", "CEN b*llocks", "God, I hate CEN", "99% of CEN stories are total b*llocks", "Someone shut them down. I'll go to Austria myself and just shut them the f*ck down".

The dislike was all the more intense, given that they hadn't been able to identify a single 'fake' story at this point. At one point, editorial director Tom Phillips joins in, not to bring a return to a constructive editorial discussion, but instead to announce he was joining in "just to add another voice to the 'f*ck CEN' consensus." And at the conclusion, when the story was finally produced, was a note to say: "F*CKING PUBBED B*TCHES."

This juvenile attitude might work among BuzzFeed's audience, but when it comes to a journalist's responsibility to be impartial and independent and an obligation to check the truth of what they write, it is staggering that this is the man who was an editorial director at BuzzFeed. It's made all the worse because BuzzFeed was claiming the moral high ground, and to be something better than CEN, yet this discussion shows they were not.

This is what happens in polarised newsrooms, where there is one set of rules for those you consider on the same side, and another for those that you consider to not share the same values. There can be no other reason for the obvious dislike for CEN by people who had never met me.

The meetings to discuss the investigation into me and my agency were shot through with cackling foul language, and personal insults, more like outtakes from a Goodfellas scene planning a hit, as they worked themselves into a vengeful frenzy with "f*cking CEN" here and "I hate CEN" there.

But really, it should not come as a surprise. Like many start-ups, they made the mistake of not realising that even if you include big-name journalists, you still won't have an effective newsroom, for the same reason that putting the best football players in the world together will not automatically give you a winning team.

They needed to learn to work together and understand each other's strengths and weaknesses. Shortly after being created, the BuzzFeed team moved from covering Game of Thrones, grilled cheese and drawing huge willies to an investigation that should have been carried out by a trusted team that knew how to work together, and if they had, it would have saved me a lot of trouble as the story would probably never have happened. An experienced team would have seen the dangers of the conflict of interest, the lack of balance and, in particular, the risks of not doing original reporting before making serious allegations that they knew were both reputationally lethal and unproven.

In the dozens of meetings and hundreds of emailed discussions about its CEN investigations, there was instead a lot of mutual back-slapping and congratulations every time more "proof" was found online to be cut and pasted into the narrative. Yet it would appear that never at any point did anyone ever ask themselves "but is it true?"

But BuzzFeed's team, even though it had Heidi Blake and Mark Schoofs, did not have a tradition in news, at least according to what was then a recent article about BuzzFeed that I found in the Press Gazette, where one source suggested there weren't enough 'grown-ups' in their newsroom. It was not so much like the kids in Lord of the Flies; it was more like Lord of the Lies.

It went on: "If about 80% of your newsroom is under 30, the office politics will be really intense," the insider said. "You do need a layer of people who have kids, and a house, and they're just there because they're paying off the mortgage. For lots of people at BuzzFeed, it was their first job out of uni. It was a really unhealthy bubble."

Having their own independent expert confirming that everything they were doing was okay had also comforted the mostly inexperienced UK investigations team, even though he was simply another BuzzFeed employee, and far from independent.

It was Smith who, when he heard about Silverman, invited him to New York and brought him onto the team, realising the importance of his independent media credentials. But despite his new role as part of the investigations team, he continued to work under digital signatures that were not BuzzFeed, signing emails for his research with his TOW Center at Columbia University and Poynter Institute credentials. As we know, the CEN project was not being carried out for either of the above. Silverman claimed to the team to be working on the project officially as an external advisor, but in fact, he was simply another member of the same team on the same mission. He was brought in as a self-acclaimed professional debunker who would show them how to take our news apart. But he had no idea either.

Because Silverman was also lacking in real newsroom experience, he was unable to properly tackle the basic question of the truth behind the material they were downloading from the

Internet. It seemed the only way to preserve his authority was to rubber stamp everything presented to him – praising them all and telling them what a great job they were doing.

It is little surprise that in such a climate, anything they found on the Internet that supported their cause was woven without question into their narrative, and anything positive was deleted and shot out into the ether. What bound them was a mission, but where did that dislike come from? The comments referenced earlier from Slack were all comments written by people who had never met me, that CEN had never written about, or done anything I could find personally to offend, and yet, they had thrown themselves into this with an, at times, almost religious fervour.

Again, it was all done even though they had not found a single item we had faked. That lack of evidence was not for lack of trying, as although I do not go into it here, I found that, in addition to scouring the internet, they had taken hundreds of our stories from the news queues of rival publications and corrupted people at the highest level in rival newsrooms to tell them every insider scandal they could. In fact, some of those people had even ended up working for them.

They had a clear agenda defined by the story's headline before they had any facts. They filtered what they found only to accept the seemingly negative and reject the positive, and if all that energy resulted in nothing concrete, what was behind them putting so much effort into publishing anyway, whatever the cost?

I wondered if one of the stories we had written offended someone powerful who was either connected to BuzzFeed and could influence their editorial or had taken advantage of the opportunity to hire the BuzzFeed editorial team to further an agenda. That is not as far-fetched as it sounds. Look at the case of Silicon Valley billionaire Peter Thiel, who secretly schemed to annihilate Gawker Media, a goal he achieved in August 2016 when he forced its founder, Nick Denton, into personal bankruptcy. The German-born, Donald Trump-supporting Thiel is among the planet's more successful tech entrepreneurs. With a net worth, according to Forbes, of over $2 billion at the time, he created a campaign as payback for an unwelcome December 2007 report in the now defunct Gawker site that he was gay. According to one book, he considered bribery, theft, bugging, and email hacking, among other potential crimes in 2011 before engaging in a "totally legal" strategy of secretly bankrolling lawsuits. So I asked myself if I had offended someone who had bankrolled the BuzzFeed story about me.

One by one, I ticked off the list until the one thing remaining was the possibility that it was never about me and only about MailOnline. That thought hardened when I found that BuzzFeed founder Peretti had been devastated when a deal he had been hoping to seal with the MailOnline's publisher had been cancelled at the last minute. The Huffington Post had tasked Peretti with a project to get them to invest. Smith wrote that Peretti had been told to carry on exploratory conversations "with a rotating series of British executives whose names he never learned". Smith added: "His pitch: The Huffington Post and the Mail could take over the English-speaking world." Peretti was proud when the Daily Mail seemed ready to invest. But as talks dragged on, a worrying decline in housing prices started pulling down other elements of the economy. Smith added: "By the summer of 2008, Treasury Secretary Hank Paulson was begging Congress to bail out key government-backed mortgage lenders. . . The

Daily Mail told Jonah that the British newspaper was out as the markets began to crater." With no other funding, Peretti was devastated that his failure to sign the deal might have forced The Huffington Post to close, not to mention the potential loss of face for failing to pull it off.

However, I put the notion that it was revenge to one side as it didn't feel right, but MailOnline was still a contender. Even without the evidence I later got from the court case, I found clues that it was about the MailOnline in other places. But it had to be more than just what was on the page, as once the King project had been published, BuzzFeed continued to pursue it like a modern-day witch hunt.

They sent queries on stories we had written to nervous clients, but never wrote anything up, with the one exception involving a repeat of a 'debunking' published two years earlier from a Polish newspaper that the Polish newspaper had misreported. BuzzFeed had been tipped off by a Polish lorry driver called Tomasz Orynski who, surprise surprise, was behind a campaign against the MailOnline, and had then travelled with BuzzFeed's Alan White to Poland to cover this not-quite-breaking news story from two years previously.

What was the story? An out-of-control sledge containing Santa had careered through a Polish town and crashed, leaving Santa and his wife needing hospital treatment. That happened, but the story said he had been drunk when, in fact, he was on medication.

Where did the CEN story come from that so outraged Tomasz? BuzzFeed itself actually answered that during depositions as part of the court case in New York. It was revealed that it was a 100 per cent Polish creation. After publication, the news site TVN24, which was the first to run it, admitted to BuzzFeed that their software had been set up to allow reader content to be published on their pages unchecked by a professional editor.

They also admitted that when an editor got around to writing up a later version, all traces of what was originally online, which was the story a former BBC reporter working for CEN in Poland had used, had been completely deleted. It underlines the dangers of using reader reporters. TVN24 did nothing to verify the report beyond seeing that the reader reporter had also taken pictures to prove they were there and that it happened, at least according to the visual image.

The fact that this story was online in Poland and was the source ultimately of what appeared in the MailOnline was of no interest to those for whom it later became a rallying call over British media racism against eastern Europeans. But Tomasz, BuzzFeed, and most of the Polish community in the UK cared nothing about the later-deleted story on TVN24, or even about CEN that passed it on, or other papers that used it. They only became interested when it appeared on the MailOnline pages.

Based in the Outer Hebrides, in Scotland, Tomasz had no personal knowledge of the story about the Santa who had crashed his sleigh other than from translating local news items and speaking on the phone with those involved in Poland, much like the way BuzzFeed had covered its story about us. Yet when they came to defend the story, he was bizarrely dragged into court as an 'expert witness'. Poor Tomasz's mistake was that he desperately wanted the story to be about the Daily Mail and MailOnline, and their suspected hatred of Polish people.

He ignored the reality, which was that it's unlikely the reporter on MailOnline who posted the story saw anything other than the words "drunken Santa," which, as it was Christmas, ticked all the boxes.

I strongly suspect that if Tomasz had known that he could not justify a campaign against MailOnline over the story and had not been paid, he would probably never have gotten involved. He certainly wasn't interested in the story where it appeared elsewhere, apart from a brief attempt to take on the Huffington Post that had used it without paying. But Tomasz never looked behind the MailOnline story to find CEN because he did not care – all he cared about was that it was in the MailOnline.

The fact that it had been sent over by an independent agency, not because it was anti-Polish, but instead because it was a strong tabloid story, and the fact that it was published in many other places, including The Sun and the Mirror, was irrelevant. The Polish Santa story suddenly found itself at the heart of the battle between the Daily Mail and Polish opponents who accused it of racism.

Tomasz was in good company with the BuzzFeed team, though. Among a mountain of evidence I found about them, there was a lot that connected them to MailOnline. The people at the top of the BuzzFeed hierarchy, for example, had learned with amazement that much of what MailOnline produced had not even originated in their newsroom, but instead was from the tiny but very influential independent network of NAPA news agencies like mine.

BuzzFeed UK's boss, Luke Lewis, who amazing though it may seem is now working for the MailOnline, was eager back then to attack his later employers. In doing so, he was undoubtedly prepared to republish anything, no matter how unlikely it was. His attitude seemed to be that anything terrible about the MailOnline was good for BuzzFeed.

His conversations with the Guardian that I obtained in disclosure shows he swept under the carpet the fact that BuzzFeed was doing the same stories as CEN were supplying. BuzzFeed's dislike of the MailOnline was evident in a look at the UK team's output at the time, with lists like '21 Weirdly Angry MailOnline Commenters'.

But there were many others, like his "Game Of Thrones as Told By The Daily Mail Sidebar Of Shame." There was some reference to other publications over the years, but the MailOnline remained its preferred target, and a list of some of the articles from the time when BuzzFeed was continuing its assault on the MailOnline reveals the bylines of many of those who were also involved in the article about CEN.

Since the CEN allegations about BuzzFeed's focus on MailOnline, there has been almost nothing in the same vein, which, if anything, further underlines that there must be some truth to the idea. Why else would the attacks have ended when CEN publicly brought MailOnline into the equation via a legal case filed in New York?

Evidence that this was the case included the 15 January 2015 email from Alan White to Luke Lewis, Tom Phillips and Richard James. The first two points are irrelevant to this dialogue, but in the third, where he outlines the case against CEN, he writes: "It looks like we'll basically show that several of our competitors have been publishing huge lies on a close-to-industrial scale. It'll really piss a few publishers off and would also probably be the end for this guy's business. It's therefore vital we're absolutely accurate about every detail: people will be keen to shoot it down. I appreciate we need to get it done, but if we do end up taking our time on something that'll be why."

On 13 January 2015, Alan White wrote to Tom Phillips and Craig Silverman, where the focus is not on CEN's fake news factory but instead outlining plans to infiltrate the MailOnline. He says: "I've messaged a friend at the Mail. She's going to try and think of someone on the pic desk that she can trust." Craig Silverman, missing the gender of the contact, assumes that going down the pub means drinking with a man and writes: "Feed him many pints and collect excellent quotes!"

On 2 February 2015, Alan White returned to concerns about this looking like a hit piece, saying: "I think we're treading a real tightrope with this piece. Because the truth is that however much we hedge it we will be saying, "Look at the sh*t Metro / Mirror / Mail run as truth and that we don't." He then adds that to get around it, it needs to look like a broader look at news production and how it's changed and "not a straight up job on him and the people buying the stories". He then adds at the end of the paragraph: "Well, not quite."

Also on the same day, Richard James, who was a CEN client for years while he worked on the MailOnline sister title, Metro, apparently without problems, as he had no examples of problem stories that he could offer his BuzzFeed colleagues, also underlines the need to keep the focus away from the MailOnline, and warns of the risk of shooting themselves in the foot.

He writes: "We aren't immune to publishing fake news / falling for hoaxes ourselves, so as long as we focus on the incredible pick up this guy's ridiculous stories get across the world, we're on firmer footing than simply screen grabbing 10 Mail stories."

The irony that BuzzFeed was also a customer of CEN seemed lost on their editorial team, even as they struggled to work out how they could formulate the story in a way that covered the fact they had been using CEN copy enthusiastically, but not paying for it.

On 12 March 2015, Alan White sent an email about CEN. In the first sentence of the second paragraph, he notes: "CEN stories have regularly appeared on the MailOnline, Metro and Mirror websites – three British tabloids with online presences that are attempting to move into "viral" news."

Given that BuzzFeed was in the business of viral news from the day it was founded, its interest in rivals doing the same was further evidence that the real agenda was to damage CEN and its clients, and cut off a supply of viral news that boosted their traffic.

He also alleges that the stories were ripped off from social media and not reported by the local news agencies in the countries concerned, which was not true, as it is a rule here that CEN stories need to be verified, and while local media is one way to do this, social media is not and never has been. It is simply far too risky.

In his deposition, Alan initially tried to claim there was no comparison between CEN and BuzzFeed, but later, he backed down and conceded that there was at least some crossover. The transcript starts with BuzzFeed's lawyer objecting to a sentence read from a version of the BuzzFeed article that went, "In the game of viral news, of which BuzzFeed is undeniably a player...."

CEN's lawyer then asked whether it was fair to say, "according to the quoted paragraph anyway, BuzzFeed and CEN do similar things?" Alan tried to disagree, but then eventually agreed we were both in the game of viral news.

However, as well as the discussions and depositions, the way a draft of a story develops can also say a lot about the influences on the authors.

On 23 March 2015, Alan White, Tom Phillips and Craig Silverman discussed how to get around the fact that BuzzFeed has also bought CEN copy.

The draft of their then-current CEN story used the sentence, "We have never been a client of CEN, but there have been times in the past when BuzzFeed did posts ab . . ." The suggestion on the table is replacing this text with "BuzzFeed, like the Daily Mail, has bought pictures and copy from CEN for posts, a list of which is o . . . "

The debate continues further down with Tom Phillips, saying: "We have never been a client of CEN", attracting the following comment: "Technically true, but may also seem misleading? I feel we should be transparent as possible with this, to the point of self-flagellation".

Craig Silverman replies, "I agree: we have to be super transparent and also inject some humility for this not to seem like sour grapes." Alan White then notes to Tom Phillips: "It's actually not technically true – we've bought CEN pics and copy." Alan White then changes the subject and suggests adding a note concerning the Mail saying that it: "has the highest traffic of any English-language news website in the world, according to Comscore."

On 23 April 2015, Alan White again felt MailOnline had not been mentioned enough. He added the site's name to the following sentence: "In February 2015 MailOnline reported that a 25-year-old thief in the South American city (sic) of P . . . "

On 21 April 2015, MailOnline and Metro were contacted for comments, and they acknowledged the receipt, with both suspicious that it was a BuzzFeed hit job. The MailOnline asks: "Are we the only publication mentioned in the piece, or will you include other publications who license CEN's copy?"

In an email on 22 April 2015, in information to staff, Robert Colvile writes about tackling the issue of CEN copy that BuzzFeed has published. He writes: "In case you aren't aware, we're basically calling out the agency the Mail, Mirror etc take all their awful inaccurate borderline racist stories from – have done a massive debunking of their work. But as part of that, we've got to acknowledge where we've used them ourselves, as per email below – plan is to put the wording below at the top of the posts concerned."

On the same day, an email from Robert Colvile to Ben Smith and a few others notes with a certain element of glee: "We also asked for and have now received statements from the Mail and Mirror, which apparently prompted a certain level of alarm in their offices."

In depositions, when Craig Silverman was asked: "Would you say that MailOnline is the competitor of BuzzFeed?" he replied "Yes". When asked how he had been researching the story when he started working on it in December 2014, he replied: "I was looking for stories on frequency and ·clients, like MailOnline, to see if photos and other details were attributed to CEN. . . " Yet when asked: "Did you ever discuss with anyone at BuzzFeed whether the CEN piece would damage the reputations of BuzzFeed's competitors?" he replied simply "No."

Likewise, Heidi Blake rejected the allegations that the MailOnline was the real target when Harry Wise quizzed her. He asked her if she had ever seen the story as an attempt by BuzzFeed to obtain an advantage over competitors like MailOnline? She replied: "Not for a second". Mr Wise then asked; "Not for a second? So you never, I take it, then advised anyone that the story ought to be made less about MailOnline because it would seem less of a hit job on competitors of BuzzFeed?" However, according to Heidi this had just been responsible journalism, telling her team to go to "all of the other publications concerned and make sure they have an opportunity to reply".

Mr Wise also quizzed Tom Phillips: " . . . you were trying to point out deficiencies in the product of BuzzFeed's competitors. Is that a fair statement?" Phillips replied: "That is true, yes. Raise questions about the quality of some of their output." Later, Tom was asked about the front-up letters where they repeated their cut-and-pasted rumours to CEN's clients: "Did you understand that by sending these letters to CEN's clients, you would be damaging CEN's relationship with those clients?" He replied: "You are aware that that is a possibility. But that is obviously not the intention, it is merely -- a natural and responsible part of journalism is to ask for comment from the people you are writing about." And Ben Smith insisted that while some of his staff regarded the MailOnline as a rival, he did not.

In his last question during his deposition in London, Alan White alone admitted that the story BuzzFeed published would have had the side effect of boosting their business. He was asked: "You spoke before that you don't believe that CEN and BuzzFeed are rivals in the viral news business. Is that a fair statement?" He replied: "That is a fair statement." But he admitted BuzzFeed was a rival with MailOnline and Mirror and that the article would criticise them. When asked if it might be "something that would be an advantage to BuzzFeed in the viral business," he replied: "I think that was a potential side effect."

I could go on; the above is just a fraction of the material I found, and in fact, the clear references here to the fact that the BuzzFeed team were aware of the benefits that the story would bring are repeated again and again. Yet the fact that our organisation was a significant supplier to direct rivals of the organisation calling us out for fake news was not something BuzzFeed dwelt on in its eventually published report, and there was no declaration of interest that one might otherwise have reasonably expected to see.

News organisations will gladly take on investigations when a subject is closer to their editorial line or of interest to readers. However, in healthy journalism, the enthusiasm for pushing an agenda that has any vested interest should always be declared. Especially when using subterfuge and deceit to gain information, which I do not go into here but which BuzzFeed used extensively with its CEN investigation, it was a PCC requirement that there needs to be concrete evidence of wrongdoing. Speculation of misconduct is not enough.

So-called fishing expeditions are not allowed when a journalist throws out the bait to catch a story. In my experience, an investigations team rarely starts a probe of this magnitude involving months of work and dozens of staff with nothing in hand. I'd even go as far as to say, in my experience, it is unheard of.

The fact that it was BuzzFeed UK's first-ever investigation makes it all the more curious. Ian Hislop, the editor of the UK's best-selling investigative magazine Private Eye, revealed in 2017 that his magazine had most of its stories handed to them on a plate by whistleblowers. Of course, Private Eye also does original research, but that could, in theory, be little more than double-checking the allegations and putting in a right to reply on top of the essential groundwork handed over by the whistleblower. However, even this groundwork was not available with the BuzzFeed story about CEN.

Unlike most other investigations of this size, it began and ended with no insider information or documents, no whistleblower to give the investigations team a head start, and no whistleblower that could provide anything of use.

It began when BuzzFeed opened up shop in London and discovered that the UK had a flourishing network of small news agencies that supplied news to their UK market rivals. They found that CEN was one of the biggest independent providers in that network, thanks to a Press Gazette story they unearthed and shared.

The entire BuzzFeed investigation, which they boasted in court had involved "three veteran reporters working for five months on the story", began with nothing else in hand other than the fact that we were one of the largest suppliers to MailOnline and several examples of our work.

There was little interest when I pointed this out. Many suggested I let it drop, but I did not, because long before the decision was made that we could not proceed to trial, the trial was no longer important. It had become just a sideshow to the investigation of BuzzFeed, not by them. One that, were it not for the personal cost, would have been one of the most fascinating stories I've ever uncovered.

* * *

CHAPTER SEVEN - SOMETHING ROTTEN IN THE STATES

Fake View

As my investigation continued, I became convinced that BuzzFeed was perhaps not the best organisation to make an allegation that I was The King of Bullsh*t News. This was further underlined by an incident in October 2014, when a Pew Research Centre survey found that BuzzFeed was viewed as an unreliable source in the United States. Their survey revealed this was how most people viewed it, regardless of political affiliation. Adweek, the US-based trade publication covering the business of advertising, also waded in, noting that most people had never heard of BuzzFeed, and many users didn't consider BuzzFeed a news site.

It seems strange that just as BuzzFeed found itself in the crosshairs of media watchers and was seen to be losing the credibility war with its UK media rivals, the BuzzFeed investigation into CEN was ramped up. Was the story about me something to distract attention from BuzzFeed's bad reputation and prove it was a genuine, hard-edged news organisation after all?

The BuzzFeed team had been discussing me in the months before the Pew report, but it was only when the Pew claims made international headlines that the discussions about CEN really ramped up into a full-blown investigation.

My problem was the opposite; we had an excellent reputation with other media, but to the public, we were unknown. That changed, of course, after BuzzFeed published their story, sending it bouncing around the world through social media channels and translating it for repetition on their foreign language versions.

My small agency, which they had so criticised, had no advertising, PR, marketing, activism, fake news stunts, or paid content disguised as news. If we had, we would not have been able to sell our content to our clients, who expected news and only news. When the BuzzFeed article was written, we had existed for precisely 20 years, doing nothing but news in its many forms; we had a tradition steeped in news.

Even our viral news was not to attract traffic; it was to sell to media partners, and that money was used to fund our quality news. It was the ideal symbiotic relationship where our investigations, best-selling books and award-winning documentaries brought a reputation that guaranteed the quality of our viral content, which could be sold for money to keep the lights on.

In contrast to CEN, BuzzFeed was founded in 2006, some 11 years later. And at the start, BuzzFeed was not about news at all – it was only ever about traffic, and the money that came with it. In fact, to say "about traffic" is perhaps pitching it too short; being obsessed with traffic might be a better choice of words.

At the start, BuzzFeed employed no writers or editors, just an algorithm to cull stories from around the web that were showing stirrings of virality. In return for functioning as a sort of early-warning system, BuzzFeed persuaded partner sites to install programming code that allowed the company to monitor their traffic.

It also tipped BuzzFeed off to the stories showing signs of virality, including the work of my news agency, which did employ journalists. I am sure it is no coincidence that when BuzzFeed was starting out we had first clashed with them for just that reason—reuse of our content without paying for it. That took place in 2009 when we discovered they had been using our stories, and I complained.

Jonah Peretti responded and told us that he was not prepared to pay, but offered to remove the content. But he claimed it would be a shame if he did so, as the content had been given to him for reuse as part of his deal with my client Metro. He implied that they would not look favourably on the relationship being spoiled by my actions.

His claim made the demand for payment more complicated, and it was put to one side pending a conversation with Metro that was never concluded. The matter was forgotten in a busy newsroom where the daily feed was always the priority.

Collecting fees from those that republish our news items was already more work than doing it in the first place, and with BuzzFeed looking like it had no money anyway and being based in the US, it was left.

But BuzzFeed was part of a new era of aggregators that, at the start, made no contribution to the news landscape while at the same time profiting from its efforts. The more I learned about them, the more obvious it became that, disturbingly, it was all they cared about, no matter what the consequences.

On the back of this, when BuzzFeed finally published its first news story in 2012, the site crashed, with the article appearing as gibberish. Smith, who had written the story, said it was because BuzzFeed, until then, had never done a whole paragraph.

Talking about the moment he wrote his first story, on New Year's Eve, he said: "I hit publish on my first post, titled "Welcome to BuzzFeed Politics," in which I promised "the first true social news organization."

"Then I went to check the page: it was nearly illegible, the lines almost on top of each other. BuzzFeed had never before published a full paragraph. While I panicked, graphic designer Chris Johanesen tweaked the code; by morning, BuzzFeed was safe for words."

It may have been safe for words, but that does not mean his words were safe for BuzzFeed.

Smith's move to BuzzFeed came after Peretti and Kenneth Lerer realised that they could no longer get by on a diet of everyone else's news, and needed to start generating their own content that their adverts, PR, marketing and other material could sit alongside.

BuzzFeed's traffic had really started to soar, setting new records every month, and their sales team was reeling in one campaign after the other, like a project for MTV for the relaunch of the nineties show Beavis and Butt-Head that involved changing the name of the site to ButtFeed. Or a deal with Toyota about a campaign that would sell its hybrid car with a post titled "The 20 Coolest Hybrid Animals."

BuzzFeed was also becoming a news site in its own right, and not just a feed of weirdness for the Huffington Post. As Smith explained: "To Kenny, news was the path to get out of the dreck of the internet, the unrefined-oil views nobody would pay for, and present your traffic to advertisers and investors as something more marketable. The answer, in particular, would be to mimic the success of The Huffington Post in 2008 and get in on the 2012 presidential campaign, in which Obama appeared to be fighting for his life against a surprisingly resilient right-wing Tea Party."

Lerer had reached out to Peter Kaplan, who had been the editor of the New York Observer since 1994, to run the show, who had declined but had passed on the name of Ben Smith. Smith added: "Kenny emailed me on a Thursday in late October under the cryptic subject line 'idea for you.' When I called him, he told me his friend Jonah, whom I'd barely even heard of, had a 'publishing venture' we should talk about. I googled Jonah, thought BuzzFeed was weird, and agreed without much enthusiasm. The next Tuesday at Lure, I sat across the table from Kenny's tall, skinny, wild-haired friend Jonah."

Lure was a wood-panelled tech-media cafeteria just down from the Huffington Post and Gawker offices that was a popular meeting point for the staff from both to exchange ideas, and after the chat, Smith had turned down the job. But he changed his mind after talking to Kaplan, who had told him: "A new media outlet defines every presidential campaign cycle. If I played it right, BuzzFeed could define this one."

So he sent Lerer and Peretti a 1,670-word memo telling them what they wanted to hear: "The biggest story of 2012 will be the presidential campaign, and it provides a perfect opportunity to elbow oneself into the main narrative. As Peter understood it, that's what you want to do.

"Jonah read it and talked to Lerer, and he told me years later that he cheered up a bit. The cure for his sense of directionlessness, it turned out, was politics. He'd loved the relevance and proximity to power that he'd felt at The Huffington Post, and he missed it; this was one of the many things he liked better than money. A few days later, we went on a walk around Prospect Park, and he offered me the job."

So Smith got the job on a promise of election coverage and then went on to deliver that. However, manipulating content to feed their readers with positive Obama news was an example of the echo chamber reinforcing increasingly polarised opinions. I've never campaigned for (or against) Obama or Trump, for that matter, and at the same time, pretended what I was writing was journalism. I want the freedom to praise or criticise either one without being accused of being a supporter. Hate the message if you like, but don't shoot the messenger.

BuzzFeed's coverage of Obama under Ben Smith as he campaigned for election and then as president was not news; it was more like a White House press release, but you don't need to take my word for it. The left-leaning media watchdog Fairness and Accuracy in Reporting (FAIR) was one of the places that looked at Smith's editorial coverage of Obama.

They wrote: "Since its launch as a scrappy clickbait site in 2006, BuzzFeed has grown to become one of the biggest names in online media and news, venturing into serious news coverage of politics and world events in an attempt to add gravitas to a name typically associated with levity and listicles. While BuzzFeed has certainly done important work of late, on issues ranging from sex harassment to AIDS in Africa, when it comes to the most powerful person on earth, however—the president of the United States—its coverage is almost uniformly uncritical and often sycophantic."

FAIR added that there was no reply when they asked BuzzFeed political editor Katherine Miller not once but twice for any notable examples of critical reporting on the White House. They added that the "continued overwhelmingly positive coverage of the president was even more glaring when one considers that BuzzFeed spent a lot of its resources documenting Russia's propaganda efforts".

FAIR continued: "One is compelled to ask, however, if a neutral observer unfamiliar with both outlets were to review BuzzFeed and its shoddy Russian counterpart, comparing their coverage of their respective presidents, how would they tell the difference?

"One could dismiss this overall ethos of flattering coverage as the mere whimsy of a pop culture website, but BuzzFeed is fast becoming a major player in news that wants to be taken seriously, and the president of the United States, despite how much we may want him to be, is not our "daddy" or our "bae." He sits atop an unprecedented global military apparatus, a multi-billion dollar drug war, a years-long assault on whistleblowers, and has waged a drone war that has killed well over 1,100 people. Lame duck or not, he's still an exceedingly powerful person, and the coverage of his day-to-day activities remains serious business.

"David Mack, nominally a straight news reporter, is uniquely sycophantic, writing the majority of the gushing headlines and articles displaying how cool, talented and squad goal–ish the president of the most powerful nation in history is.

"BuzzFeed's main investor, Comcast, has long had a cozy relationship with Democratic Party-aligned media. In addition to investing $200 million in BuzzFeed, Comcast also gave $200 million to center-left Vox and owns the generally pro-Democrat cable network MSNBC. Last week, BuzzFeed "teamed up" with Obama for a get-out-the-vote initiative.

"Its coverage of the person actually in charge, President Obama, has turned into little more press releases from the White House social media team. If BuzzFeed wants to continue to distance itself from its clickbait past, perhaps it could direct some of the hundreds of millions of dollars it's raised into aggressively reporting on the most powerful politician on earth."

Ben Smith hinted at the above of course in his book Traffic, but only by blaming others, like the Huffington Post where he did not work. He said: "Obama's supporters didn't seem to want the inside story, or to rip off his mask. They were there for cheerleading and affirmation . . ."

And that was what he gave them using something else he did not discuss in his book: BenSmithing. He is one of the few journalists whose name has become a verb, coined to immortalise how good he was at using journalism to manipulate the message. In practice, this meant that to deflect attention from a scandal or controversy, a story is written pretending to expose it. Instead, the story quietly downplays its importance, and, as if by magic, the scandal is gone—hidden in plain view.

Manipulating news for any reason has no place in a proper newsroom. When Smith was quizzed during his deposition in The King of Bullsh*t News libel case, he had clearly come around to the opinion that BenSmithing was not something he should be associated with, despite the inescapable conclusion that it is actually named after him. It's hard to wriggle off a hook like that, but it was interesting for me to watch him try.

Q· · · Have you ever heard your name being used as a verb, "BenSmithing"?
A· · · Yes.
Q· · · What is your understanding of what that verb means?
A· · · I'm not sure I understand it clearly enough to speculate.
Q· · · So you understand that it's used, but you are not sure of the way that it is used?
A· · · It was a term coined by some American conservatives to criticize BuzzFeed and me.· But I wouldn't want to speak for them in terms of what they meant about it.
Q· · · What is your understanding of what they meant about it?
A· · · You should ask them.
Q· · · Not for your understanding.· I am asking you?
A· · · It never entirely made sense to me, so it's hard for me to communicate my understanding.
Q· · · So you don't have an understanding?
(BuzzFeed lawyers object to the question being repeated)
A· · · It's hard for me to understand what they meant, and so I don't have a clear understanding.· But you should -- you should ask them.

And while that might be something Ben Smith and his colleagues could joke about around the office, in a serious editorial newsroom that BuzzFeed was attempting to become, it had no place.

BenSmithing originated out of his manipulation of content in favour of the former president Obama, and was immortalised in a 2013 article in the New York Times about Smith entitled: "The Boy Wonder of BuzzFeed" where author Douglas Quenqua wrote: "'BenSmithing is now an official term!' shouted Michael Hastings, a BuzzFeed reporter and author, at his book release party in Chelsea on a subfreezing night in January. The roomful of young reporters, ad salesmen and b-list political gadflies (Meghan McCain turned heads all night) hooted in approval. What is BenSmithing? To the Republicans who coined the term last year, it refers to writing an article that supposedly tackles a Democratic Party scandal, but is actually intended to dismiss the issue, something they believe Mr Smith has often done for President Obama. But to Mr Smith's BuzzFeed colleagues, the term has become an absurdist catchall they use to poke fun at their boss. Sometimes, BenSmithing is to share dirty pictures over Snapchat. Other times, BenSmithing is to dance a clumsy version of the Funky Chicken."

Sure enough, in the online Urban Dictionary, 'BenSmithing' is defined as:

'A political tactic that disguises itself as journalism in order to protect Democrats, most specifically Barack Obama'.
1. Something happens or is discovered that might hurt Obama.
2. That something is discovered in alternative media and uncovered.
3. Ben Smith pretends to investigate it, write something up disguised as "definitive," and then hands complicit media an excuse to ignore it.

If you are an Obama supporter, you may not feel this is as bad as it seems. Indeed, it seems that to align yourself in a camp of media that praises Obama is in itself to gain a degree of immunity for any misuse of journalism credentials.

But in practice, the danger of a strategy like BenSmithing is that the pigeons will eventually come home to roost one way or another. And this is exactly what happened to BuzzFeed when others decided to join their party.

Not only did his actions turn my organisation, which would otherwise probably never have noticed him, into BuzzFeed's nemesis, which I discuss later, but he also destroyed the credibility of the political ideology he was trying so hard to boost.

Obama was elected, but Jonah Peretti's traffic-hungry news organisations had been unwittingly training others eager to learn their secrets, such as Andrew Breitbart, Steve Bannon, or Benny Johnson.

Andrew Breitbart created conservative websites that rivalled those run by Smith and Peretti. After Breitbart's death, Steve Bannon took over those sites and became the architect of Donald Trump's political victory. Benny Johnson used the viral skills he learned at BuzzFeed to spread conservative news and comments.

In his book, Smith blamed Peretti for training and tutoring Breitbart and Bannon, but Benny Johnson was Smith's protégé, even though he was later sacked from BuzzFeed for wholesale plagiarism. But Smith had already forged him into the man he would become and created the Benny Johnson phenomenon.

Bannon, Breitbart, and Johnson learned their skills from Peretti and Smith and applied what they had learned in the campaign for the Trump presidency. As Smith was to later note regretfully, at Donald Trump's White House in 2019, right-wingers were "celebrating the conversion of traffic, not into money", as Peretti had imagined, "but into raw political power". Later, when the two met after Smith had left the BuzzFeed job, Johnson told him that he loved the new world they'd help create. He told Smith: "It's as though I had one too many shots of Jameson . . . and woke up five years later, and everything I dreamed had come true."

What Smith and Peretti had been doing was creating a mirror version of themselves, and the world would never be the same again. As he wrote in Traffic: "There, at BuzzFeed's office in Chinatown, sat Chris Poole, better known as moot—the creator of 4chan." Smith said his "angry stirrings and unhinged memes" were an early inspiration for Steve Bannon.

He continued: "There, hanging out late into the Brooklyn nights with Jezebel's Tracie Egan, was Vice co-founder Gavin McInnes, who went on to start the pro-Trump militia known as the Proud Boys. There was Andrew Breitbart, mentor to Ben Shapiro and a generation of right-wing online figures, co-founding The Huffington Post. There was Steve Bannon paying us a visit. There was Benny in BuzzFeed's West Twenty-First Street office, making lists."

The connection of Smith, Huffington, Lerer and Peretti with figures like this led to a review of Smith's book in the Guardian by the writer Tim Adams to be summed up in six words: "Be careful what you wish for."

* * *

CHAPTER EIGHT - GOING NATIVE

Ads Your Lot

You might think that Ben Smith's role in spreading activism disguised as journalism with his BenSmithing, or together with Peretti creating an alternative conservative media universe, were 'achievements' that could not easily topped, but you would be wrong.

BenSmithing has nothing to do with journalism, and he was clear during depositions that he wanted nothing to do with it, but that desire to keep it away was I suspect not because it was fundamentally wrong, but instead, because it was only a short step to another evil that he helped to enable, which was the cancer of native advertising.

It is now so widespread that it is hard to avoid. It is the process where adverts that look like news items are placed alongside news stories so people think they are reading a balanced piece of journalism. But they are not. Previously, adverts written as stories were marked as an "advertising feature" or "sponsored content", but the whole point of native adverts is that this declaration, if it was used at all, was hidden to the point where the reader saw no difference between the advert, and the article it was alongside that was a piece of real journalism.

In a world that judges media companies by the list of clients that use its services for advertising, BuzzFeed were to be the high priests of native advertising. Looking through the names, it's hard to find any significant players who were not included. BuzzFeed's commercial partners (advertisers) were like a Who's Who of the world's Top 100, including American Express, Virgin Mobile, Pepsi, Samsung, Universal, and Microsoft.

Its success came in offering a platform for native advertising that had largely demolished the separation between 'church and state', a term first used by the third President of the United States, Thomas Jefferson, to refer to the fact that the two need to be separated, where the state-controlled actions but a man's beliefs were only between him and his God. The term 'church and state' ended up being used in the publishing world, where advertisers wanted to influence editorial content for commercial advantage, and journalists wanted to keep their writing pure.

There have been many attempts to break this barrier, and it was native advertising that was to be the death knell to this separation. This form of advertising was the perfect pitch to advertisers who had always been looking for ways to publish their news under the guise of journalism.

The earliest example I could find in this battle for the news pages was reported in 1968 to the Federal Trade Commission (FTC) in the United States. It was a newspaper advertisement for a restaurant that "uses the format and general appearance of a news feature . . . [and] purports to give an independent, impartial, and unbiased view", with the FTC concluding: "Since the column, in fact, consists of a series of commercial messages which are paid for by the advertisers, the Commission is of the opinion that it will be necessary to clearly and conspicuously disclose that it is an ad."

Fast-forward to the digital age in which a whole new generation of media groups are operating from different countries with vastly different rules on such content, and it is no surprise that native advertising has once again spiralled in a new and fertile landscape, becoming so popular that I found even old-school media outlets such as the New York Times and the Guardian had started to use it. The content was supposed to be marked so that readers could see that it was not editorially independent. However, in practice, most readers failed to realise that what they were looking at was also an advertising vehicle.

A good example[16] of the dangers of native advertising involved two versions of the same story, one by CEN, published in the tabloid newspaper, the Sunday People, and a completely opposite story published in the Economist. In our tabloid story, a reporter had risked her life going to the lawless drug plantations of Albania, which were fast becoming a hub of ISIS terrorism. Previously, this illegal trade had been handled by organised criminals linked with the Italian Mafia. But many of these had been arrested in an EU-backed crackdown. Afterwards, the terrorists had moved in to take what the Mafia had left behind, and ended up controlling a multibillion-pound cannabis-growing industry. The Economist, on the other hand, in the same week, portrayed the country as both modern and forward-thinking and as setting an example for others in the Balkans region to follow.

The eight pages in the Economist had the words "advertising feature" at the top of each page to indicate that the Albanian government paid for them. Other than that, the articles had a similar style and layout to the rest of the magazine. In other words, it was native advertising. According to the country's former president, Sali Berisha, the articles had cost €1 million, and he published the Economist rate card to prove it. However, it seems they would probably have been given a reasonable discount for a bulk booking. My information from an insider is that the article cost around €300,000.

The government reportedly paid for this feature on the understanding that it would be handed out to the delegates of the then-upcoming Davos summit. In contrast, our Sunday People report estimated that the Albanian cannabis trade was still flourishing, and worth an estimated £4 billion. It further alleged that with the arrests of the Mafia figures carried out by Albanian government officials to keep the EU happy as a pre-condition to start membership talks, the drugs trade was now being taken over by the jihadists.

As soon as our story was published, it was bombarded with comments that the Sunday People story was a fake, rubbishing the reputation of the tabloid newspaper that published it. There was also an official complaint with press regulators in the UK. The level of abuse we received reminded me yet again of the quote by Oscar Wilde: "Speaking the truth that somebody wants you not to publish is journalism. Everything else is marketing."

The irony of the situation was highlighted by former President Berisha, who criticised how the Economist, one of the most respected publications in the world, had carried eight published pages praising the country's current government and its current president. In contrast, he said, the Sunday People was correct. A year later, the BBC agreed and produced the same report as the CEN journalist had in the Sunday People.

---

[16] http://www.pressgazette.co.uk/albania-leading-economic-reform-economist-or-haven-terrorist-drug-gangs-sunday-people

I am not suggesting that the Economist did anything other than follow the guidelines in the usage of native advertising, or as they called it, an "advertising feature". However, as a recent study shows, very few readers, even professionally, notice the difference between editorial and advertorial. Indeed, the Albanian report even had pages 62 to 70 reserved for its usage, making it part of the mainstream content rather than a separate pull-out and, therefore, it was not a separate part of the publication. But the real issue is that by including the Albanian government content in its publication among news, and looking like news, the question is how much would most people regard the Economist as giving credence to the claims in this content which it had not created? The advertorial claims included the fact that the then Prime Minister, Edi Rama, was a "modernising and reforming prime minister" that he was the only Albanian national sportsman ever to become a government head, and also a famous artist who has been exhibited around the world. But none of it was worth the paper it was written on, as the government paid for it to be published.

There may be nothing wrong according to the rules on what was printed in the Economist between pages 62 and 70, or indeed on other advertorial features on Albania published in news media around the world, but how likely is it, for example, that the next week the Economist would follow up the Sunday People story to confirm that there is a drugs trade in Albania, and that ISIS was involved in it? How likely is the Economist to write the following week or month that Edi Rama was a corrupt politician whose regime has been supporting the drug trade after its earlier puff piece saying the opposite? In addition, how many others might decline to write about Albania to get a share of the advertorial budget? Indeed, how many others have already negotiated deals?

I know as well as any that news is expensive. To quote the Sunday Times' Patrick Masters again, keeping journalists is like having pedigree racehorses; you need to feed them expensive grain if you want to have them on hand to win races, and the rest of the time, they are just a cost.

So, newsroom numbers have declined, and independent newsrooms have vanished. At the time, few noticed because the vacuum had been filled to a large extent with native advertising. Well written, well researched and infinitely sharable, it gave the impression of being the real news it had replaced – but it was not the same.

Author and editor Andrew Sullivan, the former editor of The New Republic, says media companies are just prostituting themselves by working so closely with advertisers and crossing the ethical line. He said: "It is an act of deception of the readers and consumers of media who believe they're reading the work of an independent journalist." Advertisers, he says, want to buy the integrity built up over decades by journalists and which, in the past, was kept at arm's length. Now, they will happily pay to imitate it: "The whole goal is you not being able to tell the difference." Sullivan was an Oxford-educated debater who gave up lucrative jobs running institutions like The New Republic and The Atlantic magazine to run his blog, The Dish. He accepted no advertising. The Dish subsisted solely on selling subscriptions, and the loyalty of Sullivan's editorial team was solely to its audience. At least, it was until it closed.

A speech he delivered at Harvard was searing. Journalism, he argued, was selling its integrity bit by bit. "The whole point of creating advertisements that look like articles is obviously designed to compromise the integrity of the system," he told the audience. "This is not a new business model. It's the oldest profession in the world. There is no... ethical line they would not cross. It is survival at all costs." And so The Dish closed, while those that had embraced the concept of native advertising were still enjoying its rewards at that time.

The fact BuzzFeed, which even allowed advertisers to post straight onto its content pages, had expanded while publications like The Dish went to the wall were mooted in the work of British author Andrew King. He argued that, essentially, what had happened with the Internet was an extremely negative development, one where large corporations have been eating each other and creating ever more powerful organisations, and sometimes these organisations that were revealed after numerous mergers had also lost almost all of their staff in the process.

This for sure was true. I have seen it all too often in the media landscape: By combining two media publications, you can halve the staff and use the same stories for each. Fast-forward to now, and the end destination is to produce a vast amount of content without staff by simply harvesting from other media. But if everyone is doing that, where is the content coming from?

With remarkable foresight, King warned as I was researching this more than five years ago that the Internet was at the beginning of this process of empire building, and as it goes on, eventually, only a few people will have enormous power. He said there would be three ages of the Internet. The first was when the Internet is free and all about sharing information and education. Then, the Internet would move into the second age, where it was purely about money and nothing else counted. Finally, he believes the third age will be one in which the big companies become tightly regulated and controlled, with governments and politicians using the excuse of abuses to introduce the regulation, and will then have control of the instruments set up by the money makers for their own purposes.

Already across the world, people are backing government laws that seem to be tackling social media abuse. But could these then be the thin end of the wedge that King warned about? But whether controlled by government or big money, the media needs to do all it can to remain independent within that system, and if there is no separation between Church and State, then what right will it have to continue to demand that independence from regulation?

BuzzFeed's success had been built on a foundation of sand that ultimately destroyed them. Those who backed them with funding were short-sighted in believing them when they claimed to have finally found a product advertisers would want, allowing PR, vested interests, marketing and activism to influence their journalism. The money came flooding in, but what they missed was that you can fool people once, but not all the time, and eventually, by corrupting the message, they destroyed the messenger. The big money then sought new vehicles, and media like the Guardian was waiting to hoover it up.

Yes, Church and State have always existed hand-in-glove; both need each other to survive. Without advertising, how will journalism be funded, and without people reading journalism, who will see the adverts? But because they coexist so closely together, whatever contrives to affect change in one will inevitably affect the other, and in the end, both were destroyed.

I haven't looked closely at how the ad agency business is doing, but how much demand can there be for their services when you can hire an out-of-work reporter or us AI to write a glowing story and pay for it to be published on hundreds of sites as a news story?

But I did look at it from the point of view of the media I worked for, where native advertising was also attracting vast sums away from media groups that might otherwise be earning revenue for their independent journalism.

As with BenSmithing, when put on the spot about native advertising by my lawyer, he was again keen to dodge the questions:

Q· · · BuzzFeed has been criticised, has it not, for running what it calls native advertising, which is stories designed to look like news stories that are, in fact, created by advertisers?
A· · · I don't think I agree with the premise of the question.
Q· · · What don't you agree with?
A· · · The second half of your question. We certainly have been criticised for many things.
Q· · · But not for publishing native advertising?
A· · · Your description -- we certainly have been criticised for publishing native advertising.· I don't think your description of native advertising is accurate.
Q· · · What is your description of "native advertising"?
A· · · "Native advertising" is advertising that is -- that is -- that comes in the same form as the media content you are consuming, like a television ad on television, a glossy page in a fashion magazine, or a list -- an entertainment list on a quiz in the form of BuzzFeed's entertainment content.· And that's all native advertising.
Q· · · Isn't the criticism of that advertising that it deceives the reader into thinking it's a news story when, in fact, it's advertising?
A· · · You know, I haven't heard that criticism in a while, but we did -- we certainly had people say that sometimes.
Q· · · Has BuzzFeed also been criticised for deleting things because advertisers pressured it to do so?
BUZZFEED LAWYER MS. BOLGER OBJECTS:· I'll let Ben answer the question.· This entire line of questioning is wholly irrelevant to this lawsuit and a waste of Mr Smith's time. He can answer the question.

Smith then went on to mention one case when, in fact, there were many.

But I did not know then that BuzzFeed had not only developed the idea of native advertising, but had also created it.

A former Google salesman, Jon Steinberg, was looking to find a company that would make him rich when it was sold, so he set his sights on BuzzFeed. Peretti had given him equity in exchange for bringing in advertising revenue, but Steinberg needed a way to turn that equity into a big payout. BuzzFeed when he arrived on the team had traffic for sure, but no revenue. According to Smith, Steinberg and Peretti came up with the idea for "native content".

They may have come up with the idea, but it was Smith who was tasked with producing the news the native content would live alongside. He was also paid to raise BuzzFeed's credibility with news content so that more native advertising could be sold.

And, of course, there are many examples of him using his news content to follow an agenda that was not reporting. Smith himself said the term "native content" was because it was "native to the web" and "native to BuzzFeed".

What he didn't say was that most people used the word native because it was native to the news content it was placed alongside. That meant it looked the same, and anyone seeing it would think they were reading news, when it was anything but news.

Smith said Steinberg saw straightaway the potential for this cheaply produced content going viral in the vast social media network BuzzFeed was creating with Facebook. At the same time, it had the advantage that it cost almost nothing to distribute. That, however, was something that was not to last.

But back in those heady days of expansion, Steinberg, with his sales background, realised it was an exciting pitch for marketers and investors to give BuzzFeed millions over the years and ignore the long-term dream of a sustainable, credible media for short-term gain.

But don't take my word for it, one person who was able to look at how BuzzFeed worked from the other side was the legendary Mark Duffy, who was recruited to write for BuzzFeed about the advertising business and was fired after a year.

After his sacking, he wrote an insight into BuzzFeed's native advertising business on his blog.

He said: "BuzzFeed is worth a lot of money, maybe USD 1 billion. At least, that's what they told Disney when the Mouse came sniffing at their hot ass earlier this year.

"BuzzFeed is not worth lots of money because of its lists or quizzes. It is worth lots of money because of its branded inline ad platform—a version of what the media industry has dubbed "native advertising"—that helps its "featured partners" (what they call their advertisers) rack up Facebook share numbers with their ad posts."

He then explains the tricks that they use, saying: "Just last week, BuzzFeed changed the layout of their ad box. Gone is the not-yellow background, replaced by a small, actual yellow box with the words "promoted by." Thing is, when you now look at their homepage, this new box layout makes the ad content blend in even more.

"The main reason BuzzFeed's ads blend in so well visually with the editorial content is because their three-column homepage layout is, very purposely, butt-ugly and busy. It's enough to make an aesthetically sensitive 25-year advertising creative vet say so in an internal meeting, with the collective response being stares and silence."

Duffy went on to openly accuse BuzzFeed of blurring the lines, claiming that it does not separate its journalism from its advertising.

He wrote: "But really: How 'seriously' does BuzzFeed take the 'separation of church and state?'

"During my 18 months working in their editorial department as an ad critic – what I was hired to be – I was emailed three times by three different staff account reps to "do anything I could" to help promote a new video ad by a then current BuzzFeed client. I was even emailed by Peretti to post about a Pepsi ad, where he helpfully included a suggested (positive) editorial direction.

"As I was still fairly new at BuzzFeed, I figured I had to do the Pepsi post, right? I didn't like the ad, I didn't hate the ad, I would not have reviewed the ad, but the f*cking CEO sent it to me! I wrote about it, positively, and posted it.

"Later that same day, my post went to the front page, and there it sat, right below a "yellow" "featured partner" ad post about the same Pepsi video—written by a BuzzFeed in-house creative—with the same exact take on the ad. The headlines were even almost identical. Did Peretti know about the in-house ad? I don't know. Ask him.

"Sorry, I didn't save a screenshot of this rather egregious church/state violation, or the email from Peretti, because I don't think like a scumbag lawyer when I'm working for somebody. But I did delete my Pepsi post, immediately. It seemed the Mad Men thing to do.

"I told my boss, editor-in-chief Ben Smith, about the Pepsi post and Peretti email, and he was quite miffed. But! This was not the only time Peretti sent me an ad to post about. He also sent me this interactive Old Spice ad, saying "a friend" of his had worked on it. I had already seen the ad, I even liked the ad, but I was not going to post about it. However, again: this was the CEO emailing me directly, so I wrote about it, glowingly.

"Old Spice was not a client of BuzzFeed's at the time. But they are now. Coincidence? Or, divine intervention?"

I contacted him for this research, but he explained that he was not prepared to comment further, and his post appears to no longer be online. But proof that this strategy was exported to the UK came when BuzzFeed's UK writer Tom Chivers published a 1,200-word post titled "Why Monopoly Is The Worst Game In The World, And What You Should Play Instead."

It started off with the words: "Monopoly is shite."

It went on: "That is my opinion, but it's not only my opinion. It has been reviewed by more than 15,000 users of the website BoardGameGeek, and gets an average score of less than 4.5 out of 10. People who play board games think it sucks. So does James Bond."

BuzzFeed deleted the post within a day. Its URL redirected to a bare-bones page indicating that "this post was removed at the request of the author" and BuzzFeed also took the extraordinary step of adding the post's URL to its robots.txt directory, a text file website administrators use to instruct web crawlers, such as Google and the Internet Archive, what not to index (e.g. any password-protected pages).

Disallow: /BuzzFeed/api/
Disallow: /tomchivers/monopoly-sucks
Disallow: /_service_docs

This means, as the website Techno Guido explained, that Google was likely to be prevented from generating a cached copy of the original Monopoly post. More importantly, it means that the Internet Archive's Wayback Machine does not possess a copy of the post and is prevented from storing one, since its crawler retroactively deletes all copies of any URLs included in a site's robots.txt file. BuzzFeed was attempting to manipulate the Internet to hide its actions. The Monopoly post was effectively invisible to any program that tracks content hosted by third-party sites.

However, after it was discovered anyway and went viral on the Internet, it was reinstated with the following message at the top: "UPDATE: This post was inappropriately deleted amid an ongoing conversation about how and when to publish personal opinion pieces on BuzzFeed. The deletion was in violation of our editorial standards and the post has been reinstated on Apr 10 2015, at 9:52 p.m."

So, as the deletion of Tom's Monopoly post shows, BuzzFeed exported its formula to the UK, where it was keen to gain a foothold in what is arguably one of the most competitive media landscapes in the world.

* * *

Smith Of Scandal

As I pieced together BuzzFeed's use of native advertising and BenSmithing, it no longer seemed so far-fetched that their story about me had been something other than journalism. From the start, it had been my suspicion that they had chosen to highlight a handful of the scandalous, too-good-to-be-true stories from among the thousands we'd created because most of them were about stories I no longer remembered.

If those claims were true, there were significant failings in how I had run my business, and it appeared I had presided over a network guilty of serious editorial failings. But it took me the next six weeks to take apart the BuzzFeed story and discover the lack of substance to all the allegations, but by that time, the damage was done; media and public interest had moved on, and my Wikipedia page was reinvented to make me into the villain. When I published my book questioning the motivation behind the story, all the accusations remained in place. By then, the media spotlight was elsewhere, and almost nobody was interested.

Nobody, of course, apart from Press Gazette, that reported for our UK partners our side of the story, [17] and did a lot towards keeping us in business. Its editor, Dominic Ponsford, had agreed to look at the book I wrote then called "Buzz Bottom Feeders" and, when finished, agreed it merited coverage. However, beyond the UK or in the quality and broadcast media, from that point on, all doors were closed.

Yet what I never really considered until too late was that even if the book I wrote had been more widely read, it was never a debate where there was ever going to be a winner, only losers. There would never be a winner because we had both unwittingly put ourselves in a category where the focus of media covering our story worldwide was on one thing only – tabloid news. It is regarded as sleazy, inaccurate and obtrusive, just some of the words that spring to mind. All that time when BuzzFeed was raising investment, when it had to list its potential threats to investors, or when anybody went online to research whether it was a good potential partner, there was the court case in pride of place. It was the battle of the two viral news giants, and once you are mainly known for viral content, you have already lost in terms of media credibility. And if you want people to put native advertising on your content, that is the last place you want to be. It's not really a surprise that after their initial success, advertisers switched their spending to more credible partners to publish their native advertising, partners like the Guardian, which also hoovered up BuzzFeed staff.

BuzzFeed either forgot, or never realised that journalism is a double-edged sword that cuts both ways. And while it no longer mattered to me to constantly have people reminded that I was the "The King Of Bullsh*t News" every time my court case was in the media, it mattered to BuzzFeed to be linked with such content.

The battle of the viral news giants for control of the sleaziest tales was the last thing they wanted. I think they had realised at the same time they targeted CEN that they needed to move more upmarket. They had tried to solve it by distancing their real journalism from their short-form news and later separated the news section from the rest of the site's content. But

---

[17] https://pressgazette.co.uk/publishers/digital-journalism/agency-condemned-king-bullsht-news-*BuzzFeed*-hits-back-126-page-defence-and-question-austrian/

it was too late, and the court case was a constant reminder of their short news, and raised questions about their quality news given how badly flawed we alleged their report on CEN was.

The reality is that tabloid journalism is simply a form of short-form journalism, keeping the report simple and digestible, and not all short-form journalism is tabloid. If properly used, short-form journalism can enrich an organisation by enticing readers into subjects they might not otherwise be interested in, and bringing many advantages to the media as a whole. BuzzFeed, in contrast, was never able to embrace this potential as it tried to keep these two forms separate, believing that short-form news would taint its long-form news and investigations, as a former BuzzFeed staffer admitted in an interview with Press Gazette. [18] They told the news website's reporter William Turvill: "There were weird politics between Buzz and News. We became the shiny new bit of the organisation – you know, 'BuzzFeed News, the real news organisation' and stuff. And every article written about the company was like: 'and it's paid for by stupid videos of cats!' And obviously, the people doing the stupid videos of cats were, quite reasonably, like: 'Hello, we actually work really hard, and the business is built on the money we're making, so maybe don't treat us like crap.'"

In contrast, CEN staff did not have this problem in the pre-BuzzFeed years because while we produced all formats, including short news and long-form, we did not publish them together where these negative effects occurred. In fact, we did not publish them at all. Instead, we sold our news individually to other media for publication. And that left us free to embrace the real power of both. Before the BuzzFeed report, CEN staff could have worked on anything from sensational short-form tales to award-winning long-form investigations lasting months or years. We did documentaries, wrote books, and, until April 2015, produced exclusive news content that has probably appeared in one form or another in every major media publication worldwide, including BuzzFeed. Despite BuzzFeed's claims, our business was not fake news, unlike BuzzFeed's business model of being paid to print deliberate misrepresentations of the truth, or rather, as BuzzFeed prefers to call it, native advertising. Yet it seems that accepting money to print whatever a client wants or to further their interests is acceptable, whereas doing short-form news means straight away that you have no credibility in the eyes of many.

* * *

---

[18] https://pressgazette.co.uk/publishers/digital-journalism/BuzzFeed-uk-rise-and-fall/

CHAPTER NINE - HERE IS THE NEWS

Cabbages And King

I carefully took apart the allegations in my book Buzz Bottom Feeders, and as it remains on sale, I have included only a handful in here to give a flavour of how BuzzFeed approached their investigation. No mention in their story was made of our groundbreaking expose of trafficked women, or of the terrorist gangs in Albania supplying drugs to Europe, or a book I wrote about American swindler Bernie Madoff's crimes committed in Austria, a work that was singled out for praise in the Austrian parliament.

Theirs was assassination by innuendo, and most of what they alleged was false anyway.

Here is what they based their takedown upon, it was tabloid content, but it was also honest journalism, where viral stories were produced that we could sell to finance our other work.

Vegging Out

When CEN clients reported that walking a cabbage was the perfect way to get over depression and loneliness, it went viral worldwide. The lonely cabbage walkers of China was, for the BuzzFeed team looking to damage CEN, a clear cut case of fake news, and nobody on their team questioned if it deserved to be there.

As a result, the lonely cabbage walkers featured prominently in the final published article, which said: "Unsurprisingly, the story was quickly debunked by Kotaku, BuzzFeed, and the Wall Street Journal. The teens were not walking cabbages because they were lonely: They were walking cabbages as part of an art event at a music festival by Chinese artist Han Bing (who has been walking cabbages as part of his art for over a decade)."

That is what happens when you simply look at online sources. We'd used links to find the story, but there's no point in simply sending back out the same story that has appeared elsewhere, and in any case, those articles did not answer the question of why. Our Chinese-speaking correspondent was told this was a top story, but only if we could get the motive, and he eventually found an item posted in China several days before our version, confirming what that was. It revealed that most of the youngsters were under great psychological stress, and don't have many friends. They were lonely to the point where cabbages were their only companions. They chose cabbages because they felt as ordinary as cabbages, which could be discarded in the trash on the way home.

This information was freely available in China on social media platforms if you read Chinese, which the BuzzFeed team did not. That report and the subsequent debate prove categorically that CEN did not invent the angle and that teens were walking the cabbages to tackle loneliness. It was already out there when the agency started to investigate, and even the artist, Han Bing himself, agreed it was not made up. He said: "It's not me who should interpret the meaning of cabbage walking. I'm playing a game. I'm the player in this game, but I cannot control the game anymore. It's your job to interpret the meaning of it." And he added for good measure: "I have been walking cabbages for about ten years. Many people ask me why, but I don't usually answer. In the beginning, they treated me like a psychopath. Now young people accept it. Sometimes, they even choose to walk cabbages themselves. They upload the cabbage walking pictures online and show them to me."

So, yes, CEN was responsible for it going viral, and yes, the CEN reporter was able to weave all the elements together to complete the story. The fact that the BuzzFeed team could not do the same, at least without anyone capable of reading Chinese, is not a surprise, and does not mean that the story was fake. In fact, BuzzFeed itself said as much when it published its previous version of the lonely cabbages story the same as other clients that had paid for it five days after we first sent it.

That version was written up by a BuzzFeed reporter who had not been told in advance the headline, so he wrote: "Beijing Hipsters Walk Cabbages On Leashes" followed by the subheadline "Beijing performance art or Portlandia sketch? You decide." The reporter that did their original story five days after CEN was Kevin Tang, and he had been so pleased with it, that after publication on 7 May 2014, he passed it on to the BuzzFeed 'world team'. That team included Ben Smith's deputy Shani Hilton.

He told her he believed it was good enough for them to feed it into their social media network for promotion. BuzzFeed's foreign editor Miriam Elder even wrote back with an "omg" comment. As a footnote – the illustrations BuzzFeed used each time they did the story were lifted from the Chinese social media platform Weibo. This was even though a frequent BuzzFeed criticism of CEN was that – err – our illustrations were simply lifted from Weibo.

Pretty In Pink Kittens

When BuzzFeed published its story about CEN, it spoke extensively about the 'innocent' victims of the agency's lies. As mentioned, they wrote: "Misleading stories built around a compelling image can have real-world consequences."

The one case they found to illustrate this point was the story of a woman named Elena Lenina, from Russia, who dyed her kitten pink – allegedly causing the animal's death from blood poisoning. For those who have not heard of Elena Lenina, she is a colourful character in more ways than just her pink kittens. She often appears in Russian news as a singer, model, actress, and author who thrives on controversy. She has posed nude for magazines, refuses to wear a seatbelt because her breasts are too big, and is famous for her many hairstyles, including one where a poisonous spider in a glass ball was woven into her hair. She also had a man as a pet slave kept on a leash for a while.

So, no shrinking violet.

After that, her next fashion statement was to have a pink kitten to match her pink outfit, which is when she came to our attention. And it was this story that put her on the international stage when we wrote that she had allegedly dyed the kitten pink as a fashion accessory and that, as a result, it had died of toxic shock.

BuzzFeed's Alan White and the team used it as an example of how our news had real-world consequences in his email enquiry to CEN demanding answers and saying: "It was covered by outlets such as The Daily Mail and Metro... The kitten was not dead. Lenina was in fact posting pictures of it, very much alive, on social media. How did CEN come to the incorrect conclusion that it had died? Did CEN attempt to do anything to restore the damage to Lenina's reputation?

"As per my previous email, I'd like to reiterate how firmly I believe it would be in your interest to submit to an interview and contribute to this story. We do not want to write a takedown (sic) of your agency, but a nuanced assessment of the realities of viral news production. It will be very difficult to do this without your input."

The language says it all. Submit? You might submit to the SS, the Stazi or the KGB, but 'submit' to BuzzFeed? Really? In the final article, White and his BuzzFeed colleagues added: "...this appears to be a situation where CEN sold a false (and potentially defamatory) story about a real person with little regard for the consequences that person would face when the story went viral. Nor has there been any apparent attempt to correct the story since it was proved to be false."

On the face of it, this is a damning indictment of the agency and its allegedly reckless treatment of the people it puts under the media spotlight. But read carefully, and you'll see that the words "appears" and "apparent" are doing all the heavy lifting. In his note, White and the rest had decided, with no proof, that the CEN story was wrong, and on that basis, wanted to know if we'd sent a correction. But we found there were more than 50 major news providers in Russia with stories about the dead pink kitten — so, as BuzzFeed should have known, it was clearly not something that CEN had just invented.

However, the fact that it was already widely reported in local media was not the only check we made. As usual, and in particular, because it was a potentially defamatory story, calls were made to animal rights organisations and some local media contacts, who confirmed it was correct, and an attempt was made to contact Lenina.

The result on May 27 was the first CEN story on the subject, "Pretty in Pink Kitten Dies from Toxic Shock".

Its important to note at this juncture that our story never said it was dead, only that people were claiming it was dead. Our story was therefore about the protest, and not about the truth of the reason people were protesting. The story was already setting the agenda in Russia, so we did not make it up, and all we really did was put it on the international stage. And when Lenina claimed that the cat was still alive, and provided images, we reported that too, fulsomely, in a second follow-up story.

So, in summary, CEN did not make the story up; it was already widely known in Russian media. As soon as there was doubt, however suspicious, CEN issued a follow-up response to the story, including the actress' claims.

With no complaint from Lenina to either the agency or any of its customers apart from her social media posts to followers, there seemed to be little need to doubt that the animal was indeed dead. Lenina didn't see the need to take it further, and why would she need to? Of course, if BuzzFeed wanted to know for sure, they could have asked her directly for proof the kitten was alive or dead. But that would be dangerously close to real journalism, not their style at all.

When Alan White, who handled the debunking and copied it over, was quizzed during his deposition, he had downgraded the story to "suggesting" the kitten was dead. Like a bizarre long-lost Monty Python sketch, the exchange with White went as follows:

Q. So the CEN story, in your view, asserted that the kitten was dead?
A. At the very least, as I recall, it heavily implied that that was the case.
Q. So in the next paragraph, where it says "the kitten was not dead," what evidence are you aware of that the kitten was not dead?
A. The fact that she was posting pictures of it on her Twitter account.
Q. Are you aware there's some controversy it was the same kitten?
A. I'm aware of that.
Q. Are you aware that CEN put forward a story containing Ms. Lenina's assertion that the kitten was not dead?
A. I'm aware that a subsequent story was published, yes.
Q. Is there something wrong with that, in your view? A CEN story?
A. I certainly don't think that it's how I would handle that issue as a news editor.
Q. In what way?
A. Well, the likelihood, based on the facts as they exist, is that you have defamed her. So I would look to be putting out a correction or, at the very least, a significant update to my clients. Was that done?
Q. What you're saying is that in addition to a follow-up story including her position, you would also issue an alert with respect to the previous story?
A. Well, we operate a different business. But if I had published a story asserting that the kitten was dead, then a significant update would be made to the story that we had published. That's all I can say.
Q. But if your earlier story had merely been an assertion that people claimed that, there would be no need for such a correction; correct?
A. It would depend on the way the story had been framed and potentially what the legal team had made of it prior to publication.

Bed And Bawdy

CEN's story of the Chinese backpacker looking for boyfriends to fund her trip around the country in exchange for the pleasure of her company and a night of passion was another BuzzFeed target.

Under the headline "Bed And Bawd", our original story went as follows: "A 19-year-old girl who is funding an epic trip across China by offering to bed a different man in every city she stops in has created a sensation on the country's social networking website Weibo. The girl - named by some Weibo users as Ju Peng from the eastern city of Shanghai - had posted an online ad looking for 'temporary boyfriends' who must be 'good looking, under 30, taller than

1.75 metres and, of course, rich'. Ju says: 'They will fund my transport to their city and all my expenses while I am there, and they need to be generous.'

"'In return, they get a whole night with me, my undivided attention, and a chance to show themselves off in the company of a truly beautiful girl.' Ju says she has already travelled all over eastern China this way and wants to see the rest of the country but does not have enough money to fund it herself. She said: 'It is sort of like hitch-hiking. It's nothing to be ashamed of.' But critics say the deal is nothing but prostitution and have called for the ad to be taken down. One Weibo user, Hsin Tao, said: 'If she was taking cash, we'd all know what to call her. This is a disgusting way to carry on'."

This story had appeared in almost every Chinese newspaper. So again, it was not a story that CEN made up. CEN was, however, one of the first to report the original story in the English language media landscape, and we made it go viral. Once it was clear that it was a PR stunt, we updated it immediately. In fact, when CEN discovered it had been a very well-orchestrated publicity stunt, that had also fooled most mainstream Chinese media, CEN sent out not just one but two updates.

In terms of checking a tabloid news story like this, apart from speaking to the girl herself and the company that sent the press release, you can't really do more than that. The fact that the firm had made the story up to attract publicity is nothing that CEN, as a foreign agency, could have easily known about, especially if local media didn't uncover the scam. The managers said it was true, and it was reproduced in good faith as such.

The next day, when the truth was found out, as mentioned above, CEN sent out an update which revealed it was a PR stunt. When BuzzFeed's in-house debunking expert Silverman was asked about the story, he admitted CEN hadn't faked it. But unlike CEN, BuzzFeed never published a correction to its article, or a "significant update" to put the record straight.

Sashimi Tapeworm

On 24 September 2014, CEN published a story that quickly went viral: "Sashimi Fan Infected With Parasites." It centred on a Chinese man who went to the doctor complaining of a stomach ache and itchy skin, and found that his entire body had been infected with tapeworm parasites after eating too much sashimi.

BuzzFeed's claim that this was fake was based on assumptions made by another media organisation that, under even the slightest scrutiny, had no relationship to hard facts, and no basis in medical knowledge.

Even worse, when the CEN version was initially published, and went viral around the world, BuzzFeed liked it so much that they again, as with the lonely cabbages, did their own version!

The high-minded beacon of truth Alan White was the reporter that had initially been guilty of shamelessly copying the CEN story from a client and pasting it onto the BuzzFeed site the next day, seemingly without a moment of concern about its accuracy. He later updated it in line with their fake news narrative to say it seems it was a fake. It appears he didn't ask himself the same questions he was asking everyone else as to why they published an allegedly fake news story.

But was it even fake?

The CEN reporter found the story on numerous sites in China before writing an English version. All these locations still cite Sashimi as the cause, and use the same pictures as CEN, which were supplied to the media by the hospital concerned. Our team also looked at broadcast media reports that BuzzFeed would have found it impossible to process because their 'international' team couldn't understand Mandarin Chinese, the world's most-spoken language. Once again, during depositions, the self-styled media fakes expert Silverman was left struggling to justify their repetition of these claims, as yet again he had not done any original research.

You Have To Be Kidding

On 17 November 2014, CEN sent out the following story entitled "No Kidding - Baby Goat Has Two Heads".

The story continued: "Chinese farmer Xu Jinkui, aged 43, was not kidding when he said his goat had given birth to a kid with two heads. Incredulous neighbours, who turned up to see the spectacular mutant, discovered that the baby goat did indeed have two heads, albeit with just two ears and three eyes, and predicted that the hideous-looking creature would not live long. Xu said: 'They told me to leave it to die, but I couldn't just do that. I asked the vet and he said it wouldn't live long either, but the mother didn't reject it and I gave it a bit of extra milk occasionally and instead of dying, it seemed to do pretty well.'

"In fact the kid is now well on the way to becoming a fully grown goat living on the farm in Sanhe village in Changle county in Eastern China's Shandong province. He added: 'It is currently 30cm tall and 40cm long and doesn't seem to show anything obvious in terms of behaviour problems as a result of its disability, although anyone that comes here can see straight away it's a mutant. I have had a lot of visitors, and some pretty big cash offers as people realise it's probably going to live longer, but I'm not interested in selling it. Maybe later, but for now, it's fun to have around'."

To the staff at BuzzFeed, this image seemed simply too good to be true, and after convincing themselves it was a fake, they contacted a digital photo manipulation expert to have this proven. Based on his report, they filed a question to CEN saying: "The goat picture that we investigated appears to be either a digital composite or a series of selective enhancements. What steps did CEN take to verify the provenance of this picture?"

Again, notice the word "appeared" doing all the heavy lifting here. Appeared is used when you don't know, and you don't know when you don't do any journalism, and simply copy whatever you are writing from somewhere else. The reality is that this story was widely reported on all Chinese media, including the state organs, and was covered to such an extent in so many places, it meant there was little doubt that it was true.

Although CEN did not speak to the farmer, the agency was lucky enough to see several TV reports with video to confirm that it was correct. There was also an interview with the farmer that provided the quotes on the story we eventually shared. All reports even agreed on the farmer's full name, Xu Jinkui.

Once again, therefore, it seems there's nothing to suggest that the CEN story was fake, that the pictures were fake, or to prove that any of the details were made up. There were others that BuzzFeed took potshots at, and some where, maybe. our work could have been better.

But nothing, absolutely nothing, justified that bullsh*t headline.

* * *

CHAPTER TEN - PUBLISH AND BE SLAMMED

Vocal Recall

It never seemed to occur to the army of BuzzFeed staff who worked on the story that all news organisations are sometimes fooled or hoaxed despite their best efforts. It should have been well-known by fake news expert Craig Silverman, who was one of the three reporters bylined on the King story, and he should have shared it with the others in the three-man BuzzFeed team: Tom Phillips and Alan White.

In fact, when it was finally published, not just these three, but more than 80 BuzzFeed staff had been involved in the story at one point or another, and I pieced together much of what they did, which all too often was not journalism. Partly for reasons of brevity, I have left most of the others involved out of this narrative to focus on these three, and I have also kept what I found out about them to the bare minimum. Yet even a small selection from the mountain of information I unearthed about this trio is disconcerting enough.

Starting off with Silverman. Heidi Blake described him as "possibly the world's foremost expert on fake news on the basis of his work" and praised his use of "some sort of digital whizz-kiddery to debunk stories".

But what does that mean? When I started looking at his career, I realised that he had done very little before his work on CEN. The only fakery was seemingly his reputation, as it was only his work on CEN that put him on the world stage and kick-started his career from a struggling freelance running a blog on news fakes.

That blog had previously earned him zero income, but after his CEN work, he became a much-in-demand guest speaker and advisor on fake news. He admits that he started investigating CEN in the summer of 2014, when he "saw someone on Twitter share an article in the Daily Mail that claimed a man in Russia had been saved from a bear attack when his cell phone played a Justin Bieber song as a ringtone".

What Silverman had done in that story was the same as what he was to do at BuzzFeed, simply copy and paste the work of others into his narrative. The real irony, however, is that the BuzzFeed news team had also published the exact same story of Bieber and the fisherman as true.

And that really is true.

Such was the level of incompetence among Silverman and the team, that it was still online when they published their allegations against CEN, highlighting the Bieber story as proof of their claims. It was not an isolated example.

On 17 April, 2015, Ben Smith's deputy Shani Hilton was involved in a purge on tracking down the stories that originated from CEN that BuzzFeed was going to admit publishing and says there are no more than ten. The ten she admits to includes the man who ended up with parasites from eating sashimi, which, as we've seen, was not a fake news story and was 100% correct. Alan White, who originally wrote that story, could have saved himself the trouble of correcting his article if he'd checked what the website fact-checker Snopes had written before repeating it.

In depositions, White was asked: "So is it fair to say that you relied on Snopes for the idea that the sashimi story had been debunked?" He replied: "We did." Then he was asked: "And didn't do any further research into whether that was true or false?" He replied: "We did not." Yet despite the lack of research, Alan White still wanted to defend the Snopes report with no proof it was correct.

Q. Referring now to the first paragraph of text on that page, where it appears to say that X-ray photos of the alleged victim were 'similar to those included in a...case report....' Does it surprise you that the X-rays of someone with a disease would be similar to the X-rays of someone else who had the same disease?
A. No, it doesn't.
Q. Do you think that the similarity of the X-rays would be sufficient to conclude that a story was a phoney?
A. I think it would raise severe doubts.
Q. "Severe doubts." So if an X-ray of a broken arm was similar to an X-ray of someone else's broken arm in a different story, it would raise significant doubts in your mind as to whether a story was fake?
A. I think the situation is a little more complex than that because there's -- it would depend on how the arm was broken or where the break took place.
Q. Do you know what the disease disseminated cysticercosis is?
A. I believe it's, sort of, internal weals from the parasites.
Q. Right. And they are distributed throughout the body; correct? That's what "disseminated" means?
A. Uh-huh.
Q. So they're all over the place?
A. Uh-huh.
Q. So doesn't that suggest to you that two X-rays would be quite similar if they're showing the same disease?
A. I think it's a possibility. I find it hard to imagine that Snopes wouldn't take that into account, given their track record.
Q. So you're assuming that Snopes perhaps had something else?
A. In this instance, I did.
Q. But you don't know what that is?
A. I don't.

The mystery deepens when you know that the MailOnline and Snopes have a history. I found, for example, a MailOnline story saying Snopes was on the verge of collapse after the founder was accused of fraud, lies and putting prostitutes and his honeymoon on expenses. Wired author Michelle Dean revealed that Snopes didn't even hire their first writer until 2014, which probably explains the lack of journalism involved in their debunking of the raw fish story that was carried out by none other than site founder David Mikkelson. He had actually founded the site with his wife Barbara, and was later involved in a messy divorce proceeding with her which involved eradicating her involvement in the project. All that information, though, was absent from the BuzzFeed report, that repeated Snopes debunking as if it was gospel.

And just to round that off, in 2021, BuzzFeed itself accused the founder of Snopes, David Mikkelson, of plagiarising dozens of articles culled from mainstream media and passing them off as his own. But his earlier assistance in helping BuzzFeed expose CEN was not, it seems, worth a mention.

What emerges in the pages of documents and discussions and questioning is a bizarre kind of osmosis in the BuzzFeed newsroom, where the only thing that can pass through the membrane is anything that fits the narrative of the headline. When found, this material is deemed worthy by virtue of providing what's needed to flesh out the story, and it is accepted as fact without question. This is not journalism; it is activism, where you find something that supports what you are trying to do, and it's accepted into your arguments for that reason only. Being true and wanting it to be true are the same thing in the BuzzFeed universe. Instead of balancing facts for and against, its only for and for. If it serves the greater good, that's all that's needed. But when this is how you assemble the facts, it's no longer journalism.

Silverman was brought in as a professional "debunker" who would show them how to take our news apart. But even he was forced to admit that despite advising people to always go to the source, he had never done the same.

What he did do was bring with him a computer programme called Emergent, allegedly able to discern true news from fake news. That is quite a claim; but is it true?

By December, he was already using it at BuzzFeed as the perfect way of debunking CEN. So how did Emergent work? In essence, for every single story, the BuzzFeed journalists were expected to put in a vast amount of information, including doing the actual work of searching online to see if they could find if anyone else had already debunked it. If they had, the team had to add the details to Emergent. So Emergent was useless for BuzzFeed's work because it simply encouraged them to cut and paste somebody else's debunking. And if it was in a foreign language, which basically applies to every single CEN story they found, Emergent was utterly useless, as it only worked in English. Silverman himself was asked to define exactly what Emergent did, if anything, and the answer was not a lot.

Q:·· Now, is this a system that could, in itself, by itself, debunk a story?
A: No.
Q·· You still would need someone to go and check out the facts at some point, correct?
A·· Correct.
Q·· Was there something connected with this project called -- Emergent called a truthiness rating?
A·· Yes, I believe our internal designation of how we were rating an article -- I think we used the term "truthiness rating."
Q·· So, it was a way to rate the article that you were entering into the system to follow?
A·· Yes.
Q·· And did you coin the term, or did you consciously borrow it from the American comedian Stephen Colbert?

A· · It was definitely consciously from - inspired by Stephen Colbert.

Q· · How did you create a truthiness rating for any particular piece?

A· · It involved looking at the content of the story itself and examining the claims that were being made about the core claim that we were interested in, and then determining what evidence it had to back that up.

Q· · So, it was basically a subjective evaluation by the person entering the story?

A· · It was an evaluation by the person entering the story using a methodology that we set out.

Q· · What would be the significance of the truthiness rating in the operation of Emergent?

A· · It was used by us, in the research, to determine, you know, the data that we had.

Q· · Could you tell me what you mean by "determine the data that we had"?

A· · Well, when we would go to analyse the data, ·we were able to look at stories that were unverified, stories that were true, stories that were false, and we were able to then compare that to things like our social interaction data that we had.

Q· · I confess I'm still not clear about how the truthiness rating worked. As you enter -- as you pick a story to examine and enter it in the Emergent system, you rate it on how true it seems or how false it looks like it might be; that's the truthiness rating?

A· · So, my recollection of it was, it was actually initially more about how the story itself was treating the claim. So, if, for example, the headline of an article said -- you know, made a claim about something and then attributed it to officials or attributed it to reports, then we rated that as kind of repeating the claim. It was them not necessarily, you know, endorsing it directly, it was them sort of propagating it with attribution.· If they did not add particular attribution, then they were stating that claim as true. If they had a headline that was clearly labelling it as false, then they were labelling it as false. So, it was more a reflection of what - how the article in question was dealing with the claim.

Q· · So, it was more, in terms - more relevant to the nature of the article than the subjective judgment of the person entering the article into the system, as to how true or false it was?

A· · That's correct, yes.

Q· · Has Emergent become a commercial success?

A· · No.

Q· · What is the status of Emergent at the present time?

A· · The website is still active, but it is dormant; it's not being updated.

Alan White, in his deposition, also admitted that the tool that was supposed to salvage their investigation and provide them with real facts did not work:

Q. Referring back to your testimony about Craig Silverman, are you familiar with a product that he created called Emergent?

A. I am familiar.

Q. What is "Emergent"?

A. It was a tool he created to verify viral news. The purpose was for people to be able to input stories into the system, and then the system's users could chip in with marks either proving or disproving the stories.

Q. So was it a website?

A. Yes.

Q. And people -- strike that. Was it used in connection with preparing the story?
A. Yes.
Q. Did it work?
A. No.

So that one truthiness that seemed to be emerging was that Emergent was as much use as a chocolate teapot. Towards the end of the project, the BuzzFeed investigations team had given up on Emergent and moved to use excels, but were still not doing any actual research.

Instead, as disclosure revealed, they were relying on a gut feeling 'light system' to determine whether the stories could be exposed as fakes. Whatever that might be, it still isn't journalism. Alan White explained it at his deposition hearing:

Q. What is a light system?
A. So a traffic light system of - I'm not sure quite how the colours correspond, but say, for example, red is debunked; amber is unclear; and green is true. We adopted something similar in our spreadsheet for the stories we were looking at.
Q. I see. So the light system is not general at BuzzFeed but was used on the preparation of the story?
A. Correct. That's just an informal thing that the three of us . . .
Q. In applying the light system to the stories that you were looking at, was it simply a matter of subjective assessment of the story?
A. Yes, I think that would be a fair reading.

White then continued to undermine the story where, as mentioned earlier, they had not only not meant to say that the news was fabricated, they had also not meant to say that the quotes were fabricated.

Q. Now, when you say "in terms of made up vox pops from my stuff, it's going to be near-impossible to ever get cast iron certainty" what did you mean?
A. I think it's reflected in the final text that we never said these quotes were fabricated; we merely said we were suspicious about them.
Q. I believe that one of the reasons you said you were suspicious about them was that they were in colloquial English or idiomatic English?
A. That was one reason.
Q. What should they be in if you're translating into English from a foreign language?
A. Well, I would suggest that the colloquialisms, in some cases - it's legitimate to translate into as close a representation of the words as possible, but we thought there were certain turns of phrases that wouldn't be used in the original language or anything like. And that raised doubts for us.
Q. Was one of them, do I recall, "straightaway"?
A. Potentially.
Q. Why would it not be likely that there was some Chinese term that was close enough to "straightaway" to justify being translated in that manner?
A. That, I don't know.

Q: What is wrong with a statement that reads like it is being spoken by someone interviewed on a London street?
A. There's nothing wrong with it. It raises suspicions as to the provenance of the quote.
Q. Why does it raise suspicions as to the provenance of the quote?
A. I wouldn't say, in my experience, it's common practice for quotes to be translated in quotes in such a colloquial way. Not when I've read other news agencies. There's no hard and fast rule with this, but that's my feeling.

This summarises Alan White perfectly. He failed to question enough, and when he was one of the few to raise legitimate concerns, he always bowed to louder colleagues and quickly stepped back into line. His main quality for his lead role in the BuzzFeed story was his desperation to get away from the day job of memes and his naivety in assuming that this was the way to do it. It's not normally a quality that a journalist will need if he wants to go far, but in this equation, it was exactly what made him the perfect frontman for 'Project CEN'.

In court he revealed how he'd first heard of CEN: "Well, through this whole early period of BuzzFeed our jobs were to scour the internet for things that were trending, and frequently things that were trending were CEN stories."

So we were frequently beating him the stories he was supposed to be breaking?

The answer is yes, given the number of times his byline appeared on stories done previously by CEN. Right up to the day the BuzzFeed takedown of CEN stories was published, we even found two of his most recently published stories were items we had sent out some 24 hours earlier.

Unable to accept that we were doing a better job, the BuzzFeed team had readily accepted Ben Smith's edict that the stories were not true, with Luke Lewis, a former music journalist made head of BuzzFeed, one of the first to voice outrage on this global fake news network over a story from CEN about a woman who spent two weeks in KFC after being dumped by her boyfriend.

He reached out to the Guardian, where he appears to have tried to get support for the idea that CEN, a major supplier to the MailOnline, needed to be taken down even though there was no evidence. Like the others in the BuzzFeed team, he had difficulty seeing that the mere fact our stories were too good to be true did not mean they were fake.

Luke raised the KFC story in a chat with Alan White, Richard James and Rossalyn Warren in early December, where he wrote: "Would be interesting with some of these to count up just how many outlets covered them, eg KFC story, must have been hundreds. That way, it conveys the scale of the demand for this stuff in stripped-back newsrooms, but it also means we're not pointing the finger at particular publishers." It was hundreds and once again, a story BuzzFeed had missed.

Then, on March 3rd, 2015, Alan White had a what-the-cluck moment when he wrote: "I actually think the quotes from the KFC woman are legit!"

Instead of leaving it in, Alan quietly removed it, adding a different story and writing: "I went with this one instead of KFC girl as we have a bit more working to show."

Luke, it seems, did not go back to the Guardian to admit what he had told them was incorrect and that BuzzFeed had whipped themselves into a frenzy of outrage over the KFC story that they had decided was fake with no evidence other than it was too good to be true.

After the chat with the Guardian, the idea crystallised of a takedown of the agency that was beating them in rival news, making sure they were careful not to be seen as "pointing the finger of blame at particular publishers", i.e. those who were clearly BuzzFeed rivals and the clients for our news.

Someone else like Luke, who was in pains to try to expose CEN, was Tom Phillips, who graduated from Cambridge in 2001. Phillips said he bravely took a stance against tabloid fakery at Metro, admittedly only after he'd left them for a new job at BuzzFeed. He was the one to reveal the conspiracy of silence, and was to later remain strangely silent on any examples that proved that claim.

Q. So is it fair to say that at that time you had some suspicions about where CEN was getting its stuff, but not what CEN was doing to it?
A. My suspicion was that they were taking material from sources that they could or should have known to not be reliable.
Q. But not at that time, at least, making it up, in your view?
A. Not in my view at the time, no.
Q. At some point in the preparation of "the story," did you say that you were going to go back to the stories you did at Metro to see if you could trace some patterns back?
A. I believe I would have done that, yes. I seem to recall.
Q. Did you try to do that?
A. I did, yes.
Q. And what was the result?
A. It was virtually impossible to do that. There was a -- Metro changed its content management system, which had the result that the vast majority of stories from the time I was there lost their bylines. So it was impossible to trace back and be certain what I had done. Also, the nature of it was such that I believe a number of stories may have, in fact, not made it in the migration across, as I recall. And, also, that the credit - for example, if there wasn't a picture. At the time CEN was not supplying pictures with every story; as a result, there would be no way of determining whether or not the story had originated with CEN.
Q. So that prevented you from doing the search that you had hoped to do?
A. By and large, yes. Although, I would note that part of the other problem was that my suspicions had been aroused by stories that I did not publish because my suspicions had been aroused. So there wouldn't have been evidence for them ever because they never made it to the website.
Q. Did you ever report your suspicions about CEN material to press outlets like Press Gazette, Private Eye, or Media Guardian?
A. No.

At BuzzFeed, Tom Phillips had made a name for himself not for his journalism, but for sharing an image of a huge penis he had drawn on the front page of the Sun, which he was later keen to distance himself from:

Q. Mr. Phillips, have you had a chance to look at a document that we marked as MM (he is shown a hand drawn picture of a phallus) for identification?
A. I have.
Q. What is this document?
A. This appears to be a screen shot of a Tweet from BuzzFeed U.K. about a piece about The Scottish Sun.
Q. Do you have any connection to this Tweet?
A. I mean, I don't think I wrote the Tweet. I don't recall. It's possible that I worked on the piece that it refers to.
Q. You didn't draw the picture?
A. I may have drawn the picture (of the phallus). I have no idea.
Q. No idea, sitting here today, whether you did or not?
A. I cannot recall.
Q. What is the purpose of this Tweet, if you can?
A. The purpose of the Tweet is to direct readers, followers of our Twitter feed, to the story.
Q. And was it a derogatory story about the Sun?
A: Derogatory? I -- from my recollection of this, this is -- funny would be my description of this.

The disclosure process revealed an email conversation string that originated with Phillips requesting fakes from colleagues. Alan White had then asked: "I just don't quite see how we are going to reach the point where you can say 'This is definitely fake'."

But BuzzFeed UK boss Luke Lewis tells him not to worry, saying: "You may not have to. Could interview verification experts, someone like Craig Silverman, and get to the point where there was enough of a question mark over the stories."

That translates as, don't even bother to ask him, let's pay him a fortune to be an independent expert, get him to use his TOW journalism credentials to open doors to interview people who don't want to talk to BuzzFeed, and then reward him with a job running the Canada operation.

Silverman may have been taken on to bring credibility, independence and rigour to the project, but what he really brought was his ability to write at the bottom of his emails: "Craig Silverman, Founder, Emergent" and "Fellow, Tow Centre for Digital Journalism, Columbia University". With BuzzFeed at the time ranked lower than the lowest in terms of news credibility, Silverman, with his upmarket email signature, was less likely to have a door slammed in his face than anyone else who could only claim to be a 'BuzzFeed Reporter'.

The fact they were gunning for me using any tricks that they could, and the facts be damned, was underlined when editor-in-chief Smith had demanded the headline "inside the viral bullsh*t factory" without any evidence that the stories were, in fact, viral bullsh*t.

Tom Phillips, who worked regularly on our stories at Metro, certainly wasn't one to criticise this idea from the big boss. Despite not turning up a single example of a problem story from his time at Metro, he wades in with this pearl of crooked logic. Tom writes: "Yeah, it's about establishing a pattern of dubiousness, you only need a few definitive fakes, plus a load of dodgy-sounding ones. In many cases, I remember from back in the day, CEN would file on stories from tabloids that in their countries were widely known to be Sunday Sport/National Enquirer type outlets – you can establish that by talking to journalists from those countries etc."

This is completely untrue, but not worth expanding on, as again, he was not able to provide even one single example, and nor does anyone ask. While I was struggling to find a place to publish a story about trafficking in children, old-fashioned journalism, Phillips was drawing a massive phallus on the front page of the Sun.

I had offered that child trafficking story to BuzzFeed, but they had decided it was more fun to write about me. However, they were grateful for the pitch: It had my telephone numbers on it, which they used to call me repeatedly to the point of harassment and demand explanations for my shoddy journalism. The child trafficking story remains unpublished, although Heidi Blake, who was the head of the investigations team into me, did mention during depositions that I "had been banging on about it for literary ages" – and never sold it.

I wonder why?

It was the second time Heidi was to disappoint me after binning the story while she was at the Sunday Times. For background, selling my Paul Foot Award-winning story earlier about trafficking in women had been ridiculously easy, I had barely written the outline and sent it to London before Topaz Amore on the Sunday Telegraph called back to say they would take it.

I naively thought selling the child trafficking investigation would be the same, but the idea of women being trafficked into sex slavery seems more appealing to newspapers than the same subject involving children being trafficked.

Usually, when you offer a story, you would seriously consider knocking it on the head if you didn't get a sale after the first two or three pitches. I had, in the end, offered this story to a vast swathe of media clients, dozens in total, more than almost any other story apart from the child euthanasia killer Dr Gross, and had also explored other opportunities to see the report published, in negotiations with The Pascal Decroos Fund for Investigative Journalism for example. But they had asked far too many questions about what would be a dangerous investigation, and it was impossible to answer without putting me and my team at risk if it were to leak. The justification for asking for that information was that they needed to get people on the ground in Romania or Bulgaria to check the details. But as I said, I had no idea who these people were, and that security risk was too much for me and my team.

Of course, I don't have any specific reason to distrust those journalists, but you don't take risks in this business when you don't need to. Even when assigned to work on an investigation for a UK partner, I would only ever know a small part of the big picture. "Investigate this individual", or "find out how that company works" was always the brief we got from London.

The trafficking in women story showed that even as a small independent outfit, good journalism can still be done, and the trafficking in children was very much a story I wanted to do. I had already been investigating the trading of babies for the quality press for years, and I was fed up with the standard 'go to a gypsy village and buy a baby scenario'. I had done that ten years earlier, and the story finally needed to be done properly.

Piecing together all the tabloid stories we had done on the subject over the years, I realised there was a market for buying and selling children, especially from Romania. Kids were being born without any identity on such a scale that they were being dumped at hospitals where they lived their formative years, unable even to be put into an orphanage because they had no paperwork. I visited the hospitals and orphanages and knew it was a problem.

I kept the payment for the investigation at an absolute minimum, I would even have done it for free, but when you do that, no news outlet will take you seriously. The fee of £2,000 was ridiculously low for an investigation of the scale planned that needed to span continents and involve numerous journalists, but still, a lot for a typical papers investigation's budget to fund. CEN managed to get the Sunday Times to agree to commission further research on a smaller budget, pending a full commission, and at that point, I started dealing with Heidi directly.

I worked with her for some time on the project and arranged for my correspondents worldwide in relevant countries to send a detailed report explaining how the network worked locally. One of my team attended a trafficking congress in Romania to get contacts, we approached a Romanian investigative unit to make contact about a co-operation, and I met a contact from the social services who tackles the issue in Vienna to get an update.

I understood that once they had all the reports from the team, they needed to get the budget rubber-stamped. In that post-Leveson era, as the Insight team told me, you needed to do almost all the work on standing up a story in the first place before you can do it for real. The management was not prepared to say yes without knowing what they might get in advance, which involved our pre-investigation in testing the water. Reports were commissioned from our staff in Italy, Romania, Slovakia and Bulgaria, outlining the angles and realistic chances of success. However, the decision at the end was that it was too expensive.

I was disappointed when we were told no. I heard it first from Johnny, but that was followed up with Heidi's unexpected call to apologise. She told me they had decided to do it the simple way, which was using entrapment journalism. I told her that as a journalist for hire, we usually accept any assignments from reputable clients, but I told her that I had done the same thing she had been planning years earlier [19] and discovered it was just inappropriate.

Offering impoverished families in Romania or Bulgaria cash to sell a child had just been done so many times before – including by me during an earlier investigation for the Telegraph – and this is not a solution to anything. The sad fact is that child trafficking is very real, and nobody is doing anything about it, cares about it, or does anything to cover it except in the occasional sensational case, like a blonde Greek baby with the dark-skinned gipsy family that was making news around that time.

There was no way I would throw away a story crying out for a professional job and replace it with a piece of entrapment journalism. I told her that I would be charging nothing for my work as Insight had rejected my idea, and I was keeping it to sell elsewhere, but that she would have to pay the freelance correspondents who worked on the story for her [20]. I also kept the emails confirming my decision to walk, and why.

---

[19] http://www.telegraph.co.uk/news/worldnews/europe/romania/1448140/I-know-one-with-blonde-hair-green-eyes-very-beautiful-you-will-love-her.-The-price-70.html
[20] When a newspaper commissions a story they agree to pay, and in turn the freelance hands over the intellectual rights to the story. To

But as I say, after the Sunday Times cancelled the project, Heidi had called me to commiserate. I was surprised when she called. I had already told Insight I was walking, and the call was out-of-the-blue in which she told me she understood my decision not to work with them, she respected it, but she was sorry that the management did not want to spend the money. She said she would keep my number and details to hand and was looking forward to working with me on a different project if the opportunity arose. So when I heard that she was at BuzzFeed, and controlling the budget, and had been so friendly, encouraging and seemingly genuine, it seemed logical to reach out to her again about the updated baby trafficking story.

The subsequent investigation that I walked away from that she did with Johnny had been a PR disaster for the pair, which bizarrely had involved a supposed gipsy couple that was going to sell them a baby, turning out to be a pair of Bulgarian undercover journalists, and they sat at the table secretly filming each other.

In the months after the BuzzFeed story, I sometimes wondered if Heidi had felt I had leaked the story to the UK media. But somehow, I don't believe that. After all, it was in all the Bulgarian media, and it would have been easy for anybody to have seen it and alert other media.

For information, the Guardian version appeared under the headline: "The stingers get stung" and went as follows:

"This is one of those crazy things that can happen to undercover journalists engaging in a spot of subterfuge.

"Two Sunday Times investigative reporters, Jonathan Calvert and Heidi Blake, set out to discover whether it was possible to purchase a Bulgarian baby.

"What was supposed to be a straightforward purchase case ended up as a case of the biter bit. Bulgarian TV station, Nova, and its reporter, sensing a sting operation going down, turned the tables on the duo in some style. The result is a hilarious six-minute video, still viewable on the Guardian [21] - in which reporter Veronika Dimitrova plays them along while they are covertly filming her.

"We are very amused by this - it hasn't ever happened to us before!' said Blake, trying to pass off the train wreck of their probe as something of a light-hearted joke.

"We have found lots of women in Bulgaria offered to sell their babies or act as surrogates for cash. How about you? We are also looking at Romania, Georgia and Ukraine and other countries," says Blake at one point in the video.

"It led to renewed, so far unsubstantiated, reports that Insight is to face the chop. But it still rumbles on."

BuzzFeed UK's editorial director Phillips, who was working together with Heidi on the story about me, didn't consider taking on the child trafficking story when she shared the memo

---

accept a payment from the Insight team would have meant it was not possible to offer it elsewhere and therefore it was stressed that no charge would be made.

[21] http://www.theguardian.com/media/greenslade/2014/apr/17/sundaytimes-bulgaria

with him, even though it was a chance to do some real investigating rather than trying to find informants on rivals to spill the beans about CEN's alleged fakery.

Despite having unearthed nothing and written nothing, Tom Phillips was then rewarded with a byline, at which he seemed cock-a-hoop.

Q. I note that you got a credit on the story. Why is that, given your apparently less than substantial involvement in the creation of it?
A. Because I did do some work on it, and I was also one of the ones who, towards the end, was, for example, putting it into the CMS, and so on. So there was -- I did do some reporting.
Q. Were you one of the people looking into any of the stories that are written about in the BuzzFeed story?
A. There may have been one or two, I believe, but the majority of the research was done by Craig. So there were -- Craig or Alan. So there may have been -- I remember, off the top of my head, whether or not there are references to a couple I did. For example, there was finding the original source for some images on Weibo, etcetera, etcetera. But the majority of the research for this was Craig or Alan.

So there you have the three slightly rusty-sworded musketeers, Tom, Craig and Alan. Yet Heidi Blake, who had been in charge, who had ordered the story to be completely reworded and then rewrote it herself, who had dictated the strategy for reaching out to me and passed on arguably more information about me from our work together on the Sunday Times projects did not get a byline.

Why?

Could it be that some primal, self-preserving, residual Fleet Street cunning had warned her that this project showed all the early signs of being a disaster?

It was hard for me to imagine she really believed the claim after my previous work with her at the Sunday Times. Her former boss, my friend Jonathan Calvert, who tried to broker a peace deal between us, tried to tell me that she was innocent.

He said that when she got there, the investigation had already picked up a head of steam, and was something that the editors wanted, and she was powerless to stop it. She was, he explained: "The new kid on the block".

Disclosure, however, reveals that whatever she told him may not have been the case. She was intimately involved and also intimately involved in keeping her name out of it.

Only those naive enough not to realise the risk were keen to be named on BuzzFeed's first UK investigation. But as well as the 'Three Rustketeers', a fourth byline was buried as the foot of the copy. Reporter Tanya Chen.

Thinking that she may have actually done some reporting given that she was apparently Chinese, and most of the stories that they targeted were Chinese, poor Tanya was selected for depositions interviews.

Q··· Now, turning to the memo itself beginning with the second page of this exhibit, at the bottom of the first page, Mr. Silverman seems to have a list of what he calls "confirmed fake stories," and in that list is listed "Woman from KFC." Did you do any research to determine whether the story "Woman From KFC" was a true story or a fake story?
A··· You are asking if I did any research.
Q··· Yes.
A··· I recall a little bit.
·Q··· What did you do?
A··· I don't recall exactly.· As stated before, I do recall making phone calls to KFC's office.
Q··· But you don't recall whether you were successful in reaching them?
A··· I can't say for sure.
Q··· Do you recall whether it was ultimately determined that the "Woman in KFC" story was fake or was true?
A··· I don't recall.
Q··· Did you do any research that you recall concerning the story further down the list -- well, the next story, actually, "two headed goat "?
A··· I don't recall.
Q··· Okay.· And the next story down, "Chinese woman offering sex for travel"?
A··· I don't recall.
Q··· And the next one down labelled "Sashimi tapeworm"?
A··· I don't recall.
Q··· On the next page -- let me just run through.· I will name the story, Ms. Chen, and you can tell me whether you have any recollection of doing anything with respect to determining whether it was fake or true.
Number one, "Aunt cuts off toddlers p****"
A··· I don't recall.
Q··· "KFC" we have talked about. Number three, "Mistress striped and beaten in public"?
A··· I don't recall.
·Q··· Next one, "Blundering boyfriend burns down college"?
A··· I don't recall.
Q··· Next one, "Wife leaves cheating husband and her twin sister naked in parking lot"?
A··· I don't recall.
Q··· Number six, "Wife chops off cheating husband's p**** twice"?
A··· I don't recall.
Q··· Number seven, "Underwear thief caught and punished by women"?
A··· I don't recall.
Q··· Skipping number eight and nine. Number ten, "Chinese woman tries to
sell her son"?
A··· I don't recall.
Q··· Next one, eleven, "Chinese man tries to kidnap wife"?
A··· I do not recall.
Q··· And do I correctly remember your testimony that you do not recall being involved with the "two headed goat" story, correct?
A··· I don't recall.

Q··· At the top of the third page of the document, the second page of the memo, the page numbered 1487, the third paragraph entitled "Suspect quote", you will note Ms. Chen that in the first dotted subpart of that, there is a parenthesis that says: "Tanya, please fill in some examples of people slash places form" -- I believe that should be "from" -- "stories you looked at. Are these places in Google Maps? Do they have any local media we can find online, etcetera?" Do you recall doing anything in response to that request?
A··· I don't recall.

Even by BuzzFeed's high standards of forgetfulness, that's an impressive display of Corporate Alzheimer's. The mystery deepens when it is revealed that she didn't actually read Chinese either and only had a rudimentary understanding of it in spoken form. But she explained here that she did have a cousin in China to whom she reached out for the investigation.

Q··· Then you say you have a cousin who you can reach out. Is that a cousin who lives in China?
A··· Yes, yes.
Q··· Did you -- is that a male or female?
A··· Male.
Q··· Did you reach out to him to do anything with respect to this CEN story?
A··· To this CEN story?
Q··· To this CEN story, to the BuzzFeed story about CEN?
A··· So in general on this?
Q··· Yes, on the story.
A··· Yes.
Q··· What did he do with respect to the story?
A··· I don't recall, exactly.
Q··· You recall that you reached out to him, but you don't recall what you reached out to him to do?
A··· Yes.
Q··· And at that same email you talk about a random note. And is it true there you are just informing Mr. White about an aspect that you know about Chinese culture and public shaming?
A··· Yes.
Q··· And that's something you knew already; that's something you didn't learn as part of your work on the story, correct?
A··· Yes.
Q··· Where does your cousin live in China?
A··· He's moved. I have no idea exactly where he lives now.
Q··· Where did he live when you contacted him with respect to the CEN story?
A··· I can't say exactly where he lived at that time. He's from the southwest region - southeast region, sorry.
Q··· What does he do for a living?
A··· I don't know what he does right now.
Q··· What did he do at the time you contacted him about the CEN Story?
A··· I believe he was in school.

Q.··At what level was he in school?
A.··I don't know.
Q.··Was he in college?
A.··I believe.
Q.··Do you think he was in college?· Do you know where he was in college?
A.··No.
Q.··And then moving to the first page of this email, Ms. Chen, the bottom, is that an email that you received from Mr. White on January 30th of 2015?
A.··Yes.
Q.··Do you see at the bottom, the very last paragraph on 6239, where Mr. White says: "Re:· Your cousin, maybe just reach out to them with the headlines of some, just to see if some Chinese stories come up." Does that refresh your recollection about what you did with respect to the cousin's involvement?
A.··No, not specifically.

So apart from a few points like his name, address, general geography in China, what he does for a living and what she asked him to do, she has total recall of the entire process.

More than any other, her testimony underlines that BuzzFeed's allegations were an artfully constructed but ultimately dim-witted lie no more worthy than the high school pranks that spawned it. And for that, they destroyed the part of our business that gave us credibility and allowed us to find people who wanted to be part of that, telling stories that changed the world.

Despite Tanya's (and everyone else's) performance, Smith remained unapologetic, even proud of the story. After trying and repeatedly failing to get any satisfaction through BuzzFeed, CEN had to take the case to court, where, surprise, surprise, BuzzFeed lied again. They said they had never suggested we made up news; they had never found a source where we lied.

Without even blushing, they claimed the very plain words used in the headline – 'The King Of Bullsh*t News' – were never meant to describe anyone as, err, a King of news that is bullsh*t.

Instead, they claimed, the headline had simply suggested that we had details in our stories that other newspapers did not. These were their exact words, what do you think?

They said Leidig: " . . . decided to play the online game as he saw it. He launched websites such as the Austrian Times and Croatian Times. He cast his net far afield to China, India, and Latin America, scouring for images and posts on social networks that he could weave a story around in order to hit up old clients with a new kind of content. It's paid off; many major news websites are regular clients. One major British publisher buys multiple CEN stories every day, sometimes more than 100 a month. At £50 per story – which is what BuzzFeed News was charged before it severed its relationship with CEN – that amounts to a sizable income stream."

And that, to start off with, is a complete lie. When we invoiced them for the promised £50, they asked if they could pay £30, and then didn't pay that either. But back on track, Craig Silverman was quizzed about it first during his deposition.

Q. · Was this an idea that you brought to the story, that financial setbacks caused Mr. Leidig to change his business model and adopt an unethical model?
A. · This paragraph says nothing about ethics.
Q. · I see. So, how do you interpret the words "weave a story around images"? · Do you not interpret those words as making up a false story?
A. · It depends. · We're not saying he made up false stories in this paragraph.
Q. · What is your understanding of what you meant - or BuzzFeed meant by "weave a story around images or posts"?
A. · Well, there's lots of news organizations, including BuzzFeed, that, today, write stories based on social media posts. · So, it's not unheard of to do that.
Q. · So, just the mere fact that you used the "weave" doesn't suggest to you that you're accusing Mr Leidig of making stuff up?
A. · No. · I think in this case, my reading of this paragraph is to emphasize that he was sourcing his material from social networks in these parts of the world.

It was the same argument taken by Alan White when he was asked the same thing:

Q. Do you have evidence that at some point Mr. Leidig's output changed after 9/11 from what it had been before?
A. My understanding is that he said that himself in an interview.
Q. That he decided to start making up stories after 9/11?
(BuzzFeed lawyers object)
A: That's not something we allege.
Q. What do you allege?
A. We allege that the type of content he was producing for his clients changed.
Q. How did it change?
A. As described in the paragraph beginning "So it appears."
Q. What is your understanding of what that paragraph means as to how his product changed?
A. I wouldn't categorize it as a negative description. It simply says that he looked on foreign social media for stories and generated his leads that way.
Q. I see. So you don't interpret "weave a story around" as making up a story?
A. Absolutely not.

At the end of his deposition, White, who was the lead writer of the story, admitted that he had never meant to suggest we made up fake news.

Q. Would you agree with me that there's a big difference between writing that a journalist has been hoaxed and writing that the journalist created a fake story?
A. Yes.
Q. Did you mean by this story -- I mean you personally -- to accuse Mr. Leidig of making up stories?
A. No. I meant to raise the possibility that he'd made up details. Which I did with him in the right to reply and I never got a significant response.

Again, writing something you don't know to be true because the person you are accusing refuses to comment on it is not journalism. Tom Phillips is keen to note he did not know where the words complained of came from:

Q. Midway down the page is one more short paragraph that I'll read. "So it appears that Leidig decided to play the online game, as he saw it. He launched websites such as the Austrian Times and Croatian Times. He cast his net far afield to China, India, and Latin America, scouring for images and posts on social networks that he could weave a story around in order to hit up old clients with a new kind of content."Did you write those words?
A. I do not recall whether or not I wrote those words.
Q. You don't recall who wrote them, period?
A. I do not recall, no.
Q. Would you agree with me that the new kind of content that this paragraph is suggesting began to be produced was fake news, fake stories?
A. I wouldn't necessarily agree that that's the implication of that.
Q. What would you suggest is the implication of that?
A. I believe -- as this is in the section that describes the evolution of CEN, I believe that we're talking about the change in the approach from rewriting from news sources in Central and Eastern Europe to sourcing directly from social networks.
Q. I see. So it's merely different sources for CEN stories, not a different kind of story? Namely, made up?
A. I mean, I don't think that implication is inherent there.
Q. Do you think the implication is inherent in The King of Bullsh*t News"?
A. What implication is inherent in "King of Bullsh*t News"?
Q. That Mr. Leidig creates fake stories, and his company CEN?
A. I think that the implication of the "King of Bullsh*t News" is that they are questionable and reckless with regard to truth.
Q. Would you agree with me that the implication of "king" suggests that Mr. Leidig and CEN produce more of this content than anyone else?
A. No.
Q. What is the implication in your view of the word "king"?
A. It is that it is a major source and that Mr. Leidig has a degree of control over his output, basically.

And finally, Ben Smith is clear that they did not mean making up stories.

Q. · · I'd like you to direct your attention to page eight of 22 of this document. And, again, there is one paragraph on this page that I will read into the record: "So it appears that Leidig decided to play the online game, as he saw it.· He launched web sites such as the Austrian Times and Croatian Times.· He cast his net far afield to China, India, and Latin America, scouring for images and posts on social networks that he could weave a story around in order to hit up old clients with a new kind of content." Is there any doubt in our mind, sir, that the phrase "weave a story around" indicates that you were charging Mr. Leidig with making up false and fake stories?
MS. BOLGER:· I object to that question.

A··· I don't believe that's what this paragraph says.

Q··· What does this paragraph say?

A··· This paragraph says: "So it appears that Leidig decided to play the online game, as he saw it.· He launched web sites such as the Austrian Times and Croatian Times.· He cast his net far afield to China, India, and Latin America, scouring for images and posts on social networks that he could weave a story around in order to hit up old clients with a new kind of content."

Q··· And what does it mean by "weave a story around"?

A··· Well, I mean, I think, you know, we try to write in very specific and clear language. And it means "weave a story" -- it just means what it says here. And I don't -- we try to be careful and accurate, and so I think that it doesn't make sense for me to try to put different words to the word that we have written very clearly here.

Q··· Well, you know what the word "weave" means; do you not?

A··· Yes.

Q··· And you know what the word "story" means; do you not?

A··· Yes.

Q··· Now, in this sentence, do those two words indicate to you "make up a story that's not true"?

MS. BOLGER:· Object to the question.· Harry, what does it matter what's in his head.· It's not a lawsuit about what's in Ben Smith's head.· This is a waste of our time. You can answer the question.

A··· No.

Q··· What does it mean?

A··· It means -- it means that he's scouring for -- it means what it says.

Q··· Of course, it does.· Everything does; doesn't it?

A··· That's seems like a whole other conversation.

So the BuzzFeed line is a bit like a man holding up a sign saying 'I'm No Killer' and then shooting someone in the head.

Traffic Jammed

It took me a week to compile this book, but 10 years to get to the point where, between running a newsroom and rebuilding a strategy for a sustainable future, I could gather together the material on which the BuzzFeed story was based.

It was all done in between running an agency that was already a 10-hour-a-day job, fighting the court case, and trying to rebuild my model for sustainable and scalable news with NewsX.

In that time, I have had to deal with the incredible frustration at all the stories that could not be covered, all the tales that could not be told, all the people that needed a voice that could not be given one. It was all the more galling when you consider that our casting down was done at the hands of those who'd also destroyed the wider media landscape.

Smith and Peretti and those in their circle had weaponised news, creating BenSmithing that was the pioneer of the idea of disguising activism as journalism, they introduced the cancer of native advertising that destroyed the barrier between Church and State, they led the drive for traffic at any cost, creating in their wake thousands of copycat sites hungry for traffic with zero investment in journalism, and they exposed all the secrets of the media to the social media giants so they could learn – and then replace them with a new type of content.

As Ben Smith revealed in his mea culpa when their actions returned to haunt them: "Once considered digital gold, as social media changed the rules, traffic became elusive and, at times, expensive. BuzzFeed's clever advertisements that once went viral on their own were gradually impacted as Facebook claimed a larger cut. New rules mandated publishers to pay for promoting clients' ads, unlike editorial posts. The costs for distributing sponsored content on Facebook varied seasonally, peaking around Christmas. In late 2018, BuzzFeed found itself spending millions on branded posts and videos, its primary revenue source. Despite generating over $307 million in 2018, the company incurred a loss of more than $78 million after spending $386 million. The NBC war chest, raised just two years earlier, was depleting. Investors, once optimistic about BuzzFeed's future, shifted their focus to the present. Peretti's board grew more restless. Realizing traffic alone couldn't remedy the situation, Peretti acknowledged the need for cuts. While he had made minor adjustments previously, such as reorganizing the sales organization and closing an office in Paris, he had spared the American news operation.

"However, by the fall of 2018, it was evident that these measures were insufficient. Peretti, stressed and thin, delivered the news in his sparsely furnished New York office. The argument that had spared the news operation before had run its course. Peretti, known for his righteous optimism, now contemplated news finding an alternate route to sustainability, possibly as a nonprofit, though the path was unclear. In January 2019, deep cuts were announced, reflecting the acknowledgement that while traffic crossed borders, revenue did not follow suit. The news team in Australia was shut down, and discussions began about finding local buyers for BuzzFeed branches in places like Germany and Brazil."

As I collected the story behind BuzzFeed's rise and fall, the claims that they were trying to do something different and to hold the moral high ground were exposed as simply not true. Everything about Peretti's background had only ever been about traffic. He realised too late that traffic of the sort that he was getting was no use without real news.

I know that because I experienced exactly the same thing with my online newspapers. When we started putting CEN's viral content at the bottom of our publications, the traffic numbers shot up. But when we tried to turn it into ad revenue, the advertisers took a closer look. They found that the stories were driven by tabloid stories, and no one wants to advertise on the back of a tabloid scandal. All the later BuzzFeed serious news stories by Ben Smith's team were just a bid to catch up in the credibility stakes and compete with the Guardian for advertisers. But they were never going to advertise, because BuzzFeed was already tainted from negative publicity like the 2014 Pew report, and from CEN of course reminding of its tabloid side, and a potential multi million pound libel risk to boot.

But BuzzFeed had attracted hundreds of millions, and had a staff of 1,700, so it's hard not to have notched up some journalism successes, in fact, what is amazing is that they did not do more. It's advantage was that the money just kept them with sham traffic that was worthless once the native advertising dollars went elsewhere. When I realised what Peretti was doing, I too knew that BuzzFeed was doomed, as I had already experienced it myself, and given up long ago on trying to monetise it.

It is the curse of tabloid news, as soon as you touch it, you have no credibility: With one exception: The news agency model. News editors that commission our news are not so squeamish over content, meaning that at news agencies it can be produced and sold where it fits and is best suited. Moreover, the tabloid did not taint the quality as it was published separately by virtue of the different media brands where it appeared. So a story about electric cars reducing pollution in California can go to the Guardian, and a sex tape can go to the Daily Star.

Nick Denton had also realised that a good news organisation needs tabloid and quality, but the public does not realise this, and nobody lamented the loss of Gawker in the wake of the Hulk Hogan sex scandal, which arguably with Denton's Financial Times background was much more a pure news organisation than BuzzFeed. Everything about what he did embraced the idea of original content and breaking news. Not just a cynical way of drawing in advertisers.

When BuzzFeed's main protagonists zeroed in on CEN, the British media world was new to them: a voracious information jungle whose inhabitants were, to a large extent, kept fed, by people like me. The deposition of Smith by my lawyer shone the first light on the BuzzFeed motives in targeting me:

Q: At the time BuzzFeed published the story on CEN and Mr Leidig, you knew that the story would damage their reputations; did you not?
A: · · Yes.
Q· · · In fact, the intention of the story was to damage their reputations; was it not?
A· · · No.
Q· · · What was the intention of the story?
A· · · The intention -- the intention of the story was to reveal a set of accurate facts about an organization that had spread false information through the media, at times really done terrible damage to people's lives as well as to the business of journalism.
Q· · · Who made the final decision to publish the story; was that you?
A· · · Ultimately, yes.· The buck stops at me.· It's my decision.
Q· · · You don't deny, do you, that labelling a journalist as "The King of Bullsh*t News" will damage his reputation?
A· · · Sorry.· Could you just make that question clearer.
Q· · · I can repeat it.
A· · · You are asking me if I don't - just the -- just the double negative caught me - just ask me the question again.
Q· · · Labelling a journalist as "The King of Bullsh*t News" will damage his reputation, correct?
A· · · Yes.
Q· · · And a story that a journalist has chosen to create news stories that are fake and to peddle them as real stories is going to damage that journalist's reputation, correct?
(BuzzFeed lawyers object)
A· · · Yes.

Q.··· And you were comfortable publishing this story that would charge Mr Leidig and his company with making up fake stories, correct?

A.··· I am always comfortable publishing stories that are true.

Q.··· And you were -- you were comfortable publishing this one?

A.··· We were -- we were -- we published this story because it was true.· Yes, we were proud to publish it.

Q.··· At the time that the piece was published, what stories did you personally believe that Mr Leidig had faked?

A.··· The specific stories that were reported in our article as having -- you said - I'm sorry.· I believe that the stories that we reported in our article as being untrue were, in fact, untrue.

Q.··· Can you recall any of those stories sitting here today?

A.··· You know, I can't recall.· But if you give me the article, I think, if I have it here, I can go through it.

Q.··· I am not asking you to review the story.

A.··· I mean, I don't recall.· I don't recall the specific details, but I would love to go through the article with you.

Q.··· We will do that. Are you aware of any evidence other than what you see in the story itself that Michael Leidig has ever made up a fake news story and sold it as real?

A.··· No.

Q.··· Are you aware of any evidence other than what's in the story itself that Michael Leidig has ever made up a phoney quote and added it to a story?

A.··· Well, you know, our reporting was -- is really substantially what I know about this.

Q.··· So what you know is what you see in the story?

A.··· Yes.

(BuzzFeed lawyers object)

A.··· Well, what I -- what I know is what I know from our reporter and what is in the story.

Q.··· What do you know from your reporters about whether Mr Leidig had ever made up a fake news story that we don't see in the story?

A.··· I don't recall specific details.

Q.··· And is the same about — strike that. What do you know, aside from what you see in the story, as to whether CEN ever made up or sold a fake news story as real?

A.··· Well, I think the story is ·completely convincing; and, you know, on that point, so I know that it is true.

Q.··· Are you aware of any evidence on that point other than what is seen in the story?

(BuzzFeed lawyers object)

A.··· I don't specifically recall.

And so the BuzzFeed money machine rumbled on, attracting millions in investment from people who naively thought they were making the world a better place, at least for themselves, by breaking down the barrier between Church And State. And so the corruption spread. But sadly, what also happened was that those who were to become the new distributors of our content, the social media sites, had no idea about agencies, and never factored us into their plans.

They were too busy locked into battles with the media brands we worked for, and even those they failed to understand properly. Instead, they turned on organisations they could understand, organisations that spoke the same language, like BuzzFeed, and in many cases,+ who were on the same doorstep. They met in person, and in dealing with them found that the content was worthless, developed ways to sideline it, and eventually to replace it with user-generated content and influencers.

The media pendulum means that as online rises, carefully prepared, rigorously checked legacy media declines. As it struggles to reach the top of the pile again, standards fall, staff numbers fall and the media begins to eat itself. Millions of people around the world are living in news deserts, with no access to news from their communities. When not closing, these papers are scaling back, going from print to online, and amalgamating news from other sources that often has little local relevance.

Alongside the loss of local media, there has been a little-reported but equally devastating loss of specialist publications, places where I used to sell content, like Railway Gazette, World Drinks Report, Pharmaceutical Business News, Shipping Weekly or World Tobacco. Or there was Airport International, History Today, Off Licence News, Medical Post and Retail Week or Teddy Bear Times, Stamp Magazine and Today's Golfer.

This list of former CEN clients was once as diverse as there are interests, and if the above and others have not since closed, in whatever form they now exist, they are no longer a source of funding for the independent journalism we do.

It has been years since we were commissioned to work for any of our once-extensive list of publications that, although covering fringe interests, were nevertheless essential filters for stories entering the news landscape.

Many national splashes, scoops and spreads have started off in these media. The most recent report on news consumption by the UK regulator for communication services, known as Ofcom, shows once again that traditional media remains on the slide.

Instagram has become the most popular source of news for teenagers, and print media as a source of news has fallen from 35% of the UK population to 24%. That's a decline of a third.[22] The tragedy is that, as Ofcom reported, while social media might be where people go for news now, most of these stories originate from mainstream news brands. Podcasters, influencers, and commentators are all feeding off the news that is still generated by legacy media.

The conditions most journalists have to work under are also not conducive to doing the job correctly. I was warned precisely how it would be when I read the fading review of the profession all those decades ago. Our success was in not caring what the world thought about what we wrote, it was about covering exciting stories, not muting them until they were so mind-numbingly boring and politically correct that nobody read them.

Instead, we'd rush in, scoop it up and send it out. Long form, short form, tabloid or broadsheet, paper or magazine, online or legacy. It didn't matter. We're professionals. But

---

[22] https://www.ofcom.org.uk/news-centre/2022/instagram,-tiktok-and-youtube-teenagers-top-three-news-sources

the never-ending rise of social media has left us feeling like polar bears stuck on the ever-shrinking polar ice.

Everyone is expected to take sides. If you don't join one faction or the other and lay your cards on the table, you become an outcast, a lone wolf. And after the BuzzFeed attack, I realised that was exactly where I wanted to be.

* * *

CHAPTER ELEVEN - BUZZ OFFED

Newsfakers

In the 10 years since BuzzFeed began plotting the downfall of its competitor CEN in secret meetings, memos and phone calls, the world has changed for them too. Gone are the ritzy offices in London and New York. And the 80 or so staff at BuzzFeed who worked so hard to bring me down? Gone too.

No one is left in the wreckage apart from Jonah Peretti, the man who I believe, together with Ben Smith, has been shown in this snapshot to have done more to destroy journalism than even Facebook or Google. Unfortunately for them, as the money was pouring in to swell the BuzzFeed coffers, I was there to remind investors about the foundation on which it was all based.

Investors don't like multi-million-pound legal cases hanging over projects they are being asked to invest in. It has a way of making that investment vanish. One headline I recall billed my legal battle with Ben Smith and BuzzFeed as the "battle of the viral news giants". Even the Guardian, quoting from court papers, wrote how BuzzFeed maliciously intended to damage my news agency, in order to "obtain a greater share of the market for viral news in Great Britain, and elsewhere around the world."

That was something BuzzFeed did not welcome, but from my side, it was inevitable. After they'd destroyed my ability to do any other investigations, the one thing I was still qualified to investigate was BuzzFeed itself. It's worth noting that after BuzzFeed News was closed, the Press Gazette did an in-depth report showing BuzzFeed's rise, and fall. Using an admittedly subjective BuzzFeed journalism "buzz-o-meter", they created a graph that revealed that in 2016, when I launched my legal challenge, it was at the same time that BuzzFeed began its spiral down into oblivion. Again, coincidence? I still don't think so.

They thought I would be an easy target. But after fighting them to a standstill in a legal battle lasting years, gradually, email by email, statement by statement, their lamentable standards were dragged out of them and they imploded, victim of the crooked landscape they helped to create. When I realised that such practices as native advertising had been pioneered by BuzzFeed, it put a whole new perspective on their story about me.

BuzzFeed had weaponised news. This explained a lot.

The court case in New York was later to be shelved on a pre-trial summary judgment motion. The court felt we had failed to prove that the things BuzzFeed cut and pasted from the internet were untrue, which was always going to be hard as the allegedly problematic stories when we were finally told about them were mostly old, and the world had moved on. Complaints are usually made within hours of a story appearing, not months or even years later. One of the reporters who worked on the Russian news BuzzFeed highlighted had died, and the other had disappeared when he stopped working for us, and we had no way to reach him. As a result, the case was stopped before it went to trial. When we appealed – based pretty solidly on BuzzFeed's deposition confessions – their lawyers produced a recent news article from the Guardian claiming that we were continuing to run a fake news factory.

They told the court it was ". . . rank hypocrisy for Plaintiffs, who continue to abuse press freedoms by callously profiting from fake news stories, to ask this Court to deprive BuzzFeed of their constitutional rights in order to stifle responsible reporting about CEN's egregious conduct."

How could the court ignore the Guardian, the paper of record?

I had guessed that Buzzfeed would use the allegation that had been written by the Guardian's BuzzFeed hire Jim Waterson.

I had requested they take it down or at least give me a right to reply, but they had refused. I took that complaint all the way to the Guardian's governing body, the Scott Trust, but because Waterson said he was innocent, they agreed he was, and that was the end of that.

The fact I offered paperwork confirming he had been connected with the subterfuge against me during his time at BuzzFeed was ignored, the fact he had been involved in helping BuzzFeed to tackle my complaint was ignored, the fact he had made no declaration of interest on his Guardian story about me was ignored, and that the story he later wrote for the Guardian was timed perfectly to be used by Buzzfeed in my appeal at the second circuit was also ignored, it all counted for nothing. Just like the fact I was not told or given any right to reply by him, even when I produced an expensive IT report by a specialist legal firm that confirmed he had not contacted me as he said he had done. He had either lied or was mistaken, those were the only two options on the table. It was all ignored.

What would the court have thought if the story had said: "Mike Leidig has been accused of peddling fake news, according to the Guardian's former Buzzfeed report Jim Waterson, who was involved in the original allegation, who had access to documents about the case stolen from MailOnline and others, and who did not give Mr Leidig the opportunity to comment."

But that did not happen, and the untimely end of the legal action might have been just that, the end, but for the fact that it showed me how media now works. Even without what I suspect are missing Slack chats and Twitter DMs, and the blacked-out sections of what was handed over, it is altogether still a damning indictment, and goes a long way to explaining why we have the terrible polarisation that we do today.

From BuzzFeed's original idea, native advertising spread through the news landscape like a plague and, ultimately, did more to destroy the reputation of the media than anything before – or after. No one will tell you that, most of them are still too busy selling their own native advertising. At the end of my research, I found out who the real kings of bullsh*t news were, those hiding behind the cover of BuzzFeed and the Guardian, but I realised it was no longer important, especially as that would involve the remaining 350 pages needing to be extracted and published from my magnum opus.

I have dozens of other names, details, email traffic and documentation, but I believe that were it to be published, it would just distract from what matters, and the problem that is already clearly illustrated here, which is that there is a vital component that should be present in journalism that is no longer practised, and nobody seems to have noticed.

What is that?

It's balance.

It is what was voiced by the Guardian's editor from 1872 to 1929, C. P. Scott, in a famous essay published in 1921 marking the newspaper's centenary: "The voice of opponents no less than that of friends has a right to be heard."

It emphasizes the importance of fair and balanced reporting, suggesting that even those who oppose a publication's viewpoints should be treated with respect and given a platform for their opinions. While not explicitly mentioning political rivals, it underscores the idea of giving equal consideration to differing perspectives in journalism.

Yet my experience was the opposite of what CP Scott envisaged when he wrote his legendary essay, and that a one-sided narrative is all too present in many media organisations hoping to ring-fence their followers by telling them what they want to hear rather than what they need to hear.

The important thing that preparing this report for Harry taught me was ways to make me and my business stronger, and better adapted to survive, and that is why my focus now is on what I gained and not what I lost. I can't say it doesn't matter, but it no longer defines me as it did before, because now my focus is NewsX. The values it has are a mixture of the old, the new, and of lessons learned along the way.

My experience has also shown that, as Sir Arnold Wesker wrote in his book 'Journey Into Journalism', what we do can only be rated by other journalists because they are the only ones whose opinion we care about. But as the Pew report made clear, and the evidence presented in this book makes clear, what BuzzFeed was doing was not journalism.

Journalists also need to lead by example, the standards we demand of others should be applied to ourselves, and more than anything this involves transparency in answering other journalists' questions. We cannot demand answers from those who we suspect of wrongdoing when we are not prepared to do the same ourselves. But the key word here is 'journalists', that means those worthy of the title, not activists.

Journalism's enormous power should only ever be used to inform, educate and entertain, empowering people to make their own decisions based on the best version of the truth available. As Smith and Peretti found, the double-edged sword of journalism that they were trying to wield caused damage in ways they had never imagined. That is something they will have to live with. That is their legacy.

The only way for others to avoid a similar fate, and to shoulder this enormous responsibility in doing journalism, is to have integrity in everything we create; to do the best possible version that we can, with the best version of the truth available, and only then can we live with the consequences.

Our more recent story on the death of a young woman after Iran's morality police held her is an example. Mahsa Amini, 22, died after they beat her and fell into coma when she was arrested for not wearing her hijab properly. Our Farsi journalist knows her way around the official and highly unofficial sources in the Islamic Republic. Her exclusive, which was three days' work, ignited worldwide outrage that snowballed into an international cry of fury, sweeping up in its path to Washington, Hollywood, and on this occasion, even Hogwarts, when JK Rowling re-tweeted it. She was followed by many other famous people, such as Hollywood actress Sharon Stone. Then came tech giant Elon Musk, who revealed he was to provide free internet access to Iran's much repressed ordinary people via his Starlink satellite.

We cover stories like this because they need to be covered, even though we often have little expectation of making much penetration with them. It could have been dismissed as just another brutal beating in a country where state cruelty and violence are par for the course. But on this occasion — even though the funeral of the Queen was filling newspapers from front to back — the story took off in the Sun, Mirror and Telegraph and then worked its way all around the world. Our correspondent who filed it and understandably does not want to be named wrote an editorial where she said: "Religious belief should be a personal choice as it has been throughout history, including the entire era of Islam. It is unbelievable that it has been turned into a political and security issue to defend that belief.

"Yes, we put this one terrible story on the international agenda, but it was just one of many examples where so many Iranian women, including myself, have suffered."

But for every story picked up, many others may not get the pickup they deserve, but that does not mean we stop. We are also documenting what happens to provide a knowledge base on which to make informed decisions for a better future. As a student of history, I have seen that human development involves an endless cycle of learning, forgetting, learning, and forgetting again. Every time the lessons were forgotten it was because they were not recorded properly by journalists. Our job is to create news that moves into the pages of history where it can be remembered and learned from to stop the same mistakes from happening again.

We do not write for the respect or admiration of friends or society. There are enough jobs where you can do that. For a real journalist, the chance to have a say and be read is reward enough. The Hollywood glamour that invariably makes the film's hero a lowly reporter before achieving riches and fame after a great story is not reflected in the reality of the job, and we should not do it for that. We do it to give people a voice because we have the right to ask the questions they want answered, and hold not just others to account, but also, when needed, ourselves.

But this journey was not wasted. The lessons learned on how to stay in business and bullet-proof me and my journalism against allegations in the future are the lessons that helped to form NewsX, a movement that will stand up for the rights of the forgotten minority in the decimation of the news landscape, the journalists. Like many in the trade, I've never taken money from advertisers to write something and pretend that it's true.

I trained for two years to become a journalist, learned shorthand, studied law, found out how government works, what you can and can't say, how to be balanced and all the human skills needed to let you talk to people in often desperate situations. That was the start, and then I spent years pressure testing those skills in the field. But now, as any freelancer will tell you, it's hard to even give stories away.

Professionals who care about what they say and do find themselves in a race to the bottom with fake news and social media suppliers who couldn't give a rat's whether a story is right or wrong, just how popular. For as long as I can remember, only 20% of what I wrote was ever published because I choose not to have my own platform and instead rely on others to publish that content and pay for it.

Alongside NewsX to create content, I created QC[23] to monitor media that is not otherwise regulated as an alternative to costly legal proceedings and to give a voice to other victims of similar attacks on some of the vast fiction machines that have sprung up. Even if it's too late to help my case, with our first QC story I discovered how a vast network of Google-backed content machines are each pumping out tens of thousands of such stories every hour with no editorial staff.

Google in its wisdom does not regard what we produce as news, and prefers to offer the meagre share of the ad revenue we generate to those that rip our content and publish it as their own.

I can't even give stories away and post them online because Google doesn't recognise them as news. It refuses to give my website for unpublished content Google News status, pointing out that I can always post on Medium or Substack with millions of other people.

It has been able to ignore us because we don't have a community. That changes now. My BuzzFeed journey has shown me that when we needed it most, nobody was there to do it for us. NewsX and the 'unregulated media' monitor QC were created to change that for others.

They aim to provide journalists with a living wage and pick up the fight to make sure that what we create sets a standard that earns public trust in what we write. It gives creators a technology to support what they do with a platform to network and support each other, and criticise each other. Above all, it restores something that seems to have been forgotten, which is a code of conduct that should guide everything we write.

Journalism once stood outside the influence of politics and commercial vested interests. Now, especially online, it seems to just ask people to form an orderly queue while nakedly self-serving piffle is paraded in front of them as news.

The news media could once offer solid, reliable, independent facts to help readers make tough decisions about every aspect of their lives, from big decisions like how we relate to issues of religion, race, gender, careers or schools to what restaurant to visit. However, decisions are now more likely to be made on the strength of a one-minute TikTok clip.

But most importantly, this is not a project that is open to investors. We don't want their money and instead have created the NewsX Newshound, a trademarked memecoin to fund our global newsroom network and the independent journalism it will create for publication in mainstream media titles. And as NewsX is a social enterprise registered as a Community Interest Company (CIC) it ensures that everything we earn will be used to pay more journalists to do more journalism, not for dividends.

---

[23] https://pressgazette.co.uk/media_law/guardian-complainant-watchdog-unregulated-media-cen-leidig-buzzfeed/

Credibility is the only currency that counts, guaranteed by an iron-clad code, guided by software, and networked with each other. This story, then, is the genesis of NewsX. It took me a decade of painful experience and incredible frustration at all the stories that could not be covered, all the tales that could not be told.

There is some irony in the fact that this journey and what happened to me and my agency, CEN, happened at the hands of those who also destroyed the wider media landscape. This book is proof of that and, at the same time, a blueprint for how media can work in this new age for both news consumers and content creators. This, then, is the NewsX vision for a better way of reporting the world, told in the one way it should be told, with who, what, where when and why, and not with who cares, and how much.

* * *

CHAPTER TWELVE - WAY TO GO

NewsX ™

What you have read here is a slimmed down Wegovy version with just 50,000 words of what is a 260,000 page magnum opus detailing the activities of BuzzFeed, its staff and its partners in the creation of the story about me, its consequences, and the wider implications for the media. I knew that if I were to publish the whole saga, it would most likely not be read, even though much of the information contained there is even more damning than what's presented here. But no more is needed, the objective was to show that we never were a fake news factory, and that we never took money to write anything that was not true, unlike BuzzFeed.

When Alan White called pretending that he wanted to write a story about my 'laudable investigative journalism', and hiding what he was really planning to write, I asked him if they could wait six months for the project to be finished. He never did, because it was never what he was really interested in.

As a result, when they published their story, I lost the investment that would have completed the project, and I tried other sources of funding like Google, but when you're the 'King of Bullsh*t News' you don't get past the first hurdle. So I funded it myself spending everything we had earned over 20 years as one of the UK's leading private news agencies.

Now, ten years on, despite the BuzzFeed accusations, despite fighting a crippling court case, despite needing to find hundreds of thousands to pay the software costs to create a virtual newsroom, we are through beta testing and our global newsroom is alive.

There is still a long way to go, and it may not survive, but I'm glad that I never gave up on the dream, and I realised it to the point where now others need to get involved, and that is out of my hands.

I've done what I can, I've passed on the message, I can't control if you want to listen, and if it doesn't work, I will not be the bitter person I would have been if I had given up five years ago.

And I am sure you will agree, if I pull it off, going from being 'The King of Bullsh*t News' back to creating a global newsroom to restore credibility to the fractured media landscape will be a comeback that will make a great Netflix story.

We never had advertisers or investors, and more importantly, all the money that we earned, even from selling viral content that not everybody likes, was used to do real journalism. Anything that was earned in that time was used to keep the business alive, fight the BuzzFeed allegations, and create something new to create a sustainable and scalable journalism model.

It's also to make sure nobody else has to go through the enormous devastation an unfair allegation of running a fake news factory can create. Nothing worth having is easy to get, and the journey here has come at a heavy price, but one almost worth paying given the potential for change at the end. I was, in any case, in part compensated by getting the chance to work on a story like this. Either way, I've done what I can, what happens now is out of my hands.

If NewsX fulfils its potential as a global publisher, it will have journalism to keep it in check. If the world rejects the idea, I believe we've taken the first step to correct the wrong direction things have taken. Even if NewsX does not go further, I hope it will still influence what is to come with the revelations here about the forces that shaped it. I shared the full version of the book with a few people before publication, with one young journalist in particular reading it cover to cover, and emerging full of the potential for a new beginning.

She told me: "I really like it, it gives back a lot that we have lost, it could really make a difference."

She then paused, before adding: "But what if nobody believes it?

I replied simply: "Somebody already does."

* * *

AND FINALLY

If you want to join the NewsX project for a sustainable and scalable independent news media, then feel free to visit our website newsx.media, where you can also download our blue paper for change. We want to sign up journalists to produce content, publishers looking for exclusive news at no charge, and people who want to provide us with content that can be put under the lens of journalism in one our NewsX communities, and then published.

Our NewsX Newshound is a trademarked memecoin for global newsrooms created to fund independent journalism in mainstream media titles.

X: https://twitter.com/newsxhound

YouTube: https://www.youtube.com/@NewsXvideos

Telegram: https://t.me/newsxhound

Contract Address: HJeMAK59qX6DwFSr9uxYJnhHKBxn4NKuzfsFCYm2XLv6

* * *

Appendix Of Documents

And what a debut post.

On 25 Apr 2015 11:41 am, "Robert Colvile" wrote:

+Heidi

I'd say there a few things we want to do...

- Try to stir up wider interest. e.g. with Roy Greenslade and other media commentators

- Find out what Press Gazette were smoking (not so urgent, this one)

- Pursue the JWB angle

- Ask that CEN gives us the details of its internal investigation, or even do a breakout news post on that

- Demand that it appoints an independent figure to review its output?

- Keep collecting examples as time permits

- Check with the Mail/Mirror what their conclusion is, and whether they'll carry on using its content

Any other thoughts? Judging by the internal review line, they're trying to tough it out, so we're in for the long haul...

Rob

On 25 April 2015 at 11:19, Luke Lewis wrote:

So, what comes next? How do we follow up, keep up the pressure? If any one of these publishers DOESN'T immediately stop dealing with CEN it looks terrible for them. Should we ring round on Monday?

--

Robert Colvile | News Director

BuzzFeed: The Social News and Entertainment Company

40 Argyll Street, London, W1F 7EB

--

CONFIDENTIAL

From: Alan White [alan.white@buzzfeed.com]
Sent: 3/26/2015 4:34:37 AM
To: Tom Phillips [tom.phillips@buzzfeed.com]
Subject: Re: Fwd: Touching base

[shruggy]

On Thu, Mar 26, 2015 at 8:33 AM, Tom Phillips <tom.phillips@buzzfeed.com> wrote:

Is there any evidence, do you think, that any of these investigations of his ever saw the light of day?

On 26 Mar 2015 08:29, "Tom Phillips" <tom.phillips@buzzfeed.com> wrote:

Blimey

On 25 Mar 2015 20:22, "Alan White" <alan.white@buzzfeed.com> wrote:

Crikey.

---------- Forwarded message ----------
From: Heidi Blake <heidi.blake@buzzfeed.com>
Date: Wed, Mar 25, 2015 at 7:57 PM
Subject: Fwd: Touching base
To: Alan White <alan.white@buzzfeed.com>, Robert Colvile <robert.colvile@buzzfeed.com>

In confidence, dug out this email from Leidig ... We spoke last year about a big investigation he was doing into child trafficking and he got in touch on LinkedIn to see if it might work for BuzzFeed & followed up by email. Interesting that he leapt to defend the 'tabloid' stories they do without me even asking about them – and says that they churn those out to drum up funding for their investigations. I never got round to responding to this but in light of your stuff it's quite interesting ...

Heidi Blake | UK Investigations Editor

BuzzFeed News

40 Argyll Street,

London, W1F 7EB

@HeidilBlake <https://twitter.com/HeidilBlake>

---------- Forwarded message ----------
From: Michael Leidig <editor@cen.at>
Date: Wed, Jan 14, 2015 at 6:00 PM
Subject: RE: Touching base
To: heidi.blake@buzzfeed.com

Yes we already do a lot of work for buzzfeed but not anything you'd be interested in, it's the tabloid stories that provide the funding for everything else we do.

From:	Heidi Blake [heidi.blake@buzzfeed.com]
Sent:	4/12/2015 10:52:26 PM
To:	Alan White [alan.white@buzzfeed.com]
CC:	Craig Silverman [silvermancraig@gmail.com]; Luke Lewis [luke.lewis@buzzfeed.com]; Tom Phillips [tom.phillips@buzzfeed.com]
Subject:	Re: No surprises letter

Hello from LA!

I've taken a look at the front up letter and my suggested redraft is below. Very happy to discuss the reasoning behind the changes on the phone if you want to give me a call any time during waking hours here! The main point is that I think we need to give him much more detail about the reasons we have deduced that each article or quotation is fake to give him a chance to point out any holes in our workings. My changes are in red and I've added what I think is the requisite amount of detail for the first two examples so you can see what I mean — I'd suggest you do the same for all the other bullet points too.

My advice is also to go to every other outlet that we name in the story as having bought dodgy content from CEN, giving them links to the offending stories and a brief outline of why they're wrong.

Give me a shout if any questions!

Heidi

Dear Mr Leidig,

Following my earlier emails and our previous conversations on the phone, I wanted to notify you that BuzzFeed News is now preparing to publish an article which will report that your news agency, CEN, is responsible for the circulation of a string of stories which have subsequently been proven false either in part or in their entirety. As previously stated, I would welcome the opportunity to discuss this with you in order to give you the fullest possible opportunity to respond to what we at present plan to report. As I have mentioned previously, I understand that you are producing this viral content for sale in order to fund your laudable investigative journalism into the issue of child trafficking in Europe, and I am keen to reflect this fact in the article. However, in the course of my research I have uncovered numerous substantive inaccuracies and distortions in CEN content which has been sold on to other outlets around the world. I intend to report on this disturbing pattern as a matter of legitimate public interest and concern, and I would be grateful for your response to the points raised below.

1.
In August 2014, CEN sold a story about a man who was apparently saved from a bear attack by a Justin Bieber ringtone on his phone. This was bought by the following outlets around the world: <http://www.dailymail.co.uk/news/article-2716479/Fisherman-saved-bear-attack-Justin-Bieber-ringtone-went-mauled-scared-bear-away.html> Daily Mail, <http://nypost.com/2014/08/05/justin-bieber-saves-man-from-bear-attack/> New York Post, <http://www.smh.com.au/lifestyle/life/justin-bieber-ringtone-saves-russian-man-from-bear-attack-20140807-101cpc.html> Sydney Morning Herald, <http://www.nydailynews.com/news/world/justin-bieber-ringtone-saves-man-bear-article-1.1893607> New York Daily News, <http://www.express.co.uk/news/uk/495861/Man-saved-from-bear-thanks-to-Justin-Bieber> Daily Express, <http://www.mirror.co.uk/3am/celebrity-news/justin-bieber-scares-grizzly-bear-3995326> Daily Mirror. But the original story about the bear attack, <http://www.kp.ru/daily/26263.4/3141355/> which was published in Russia's Komsomolskaya Pravda, said nothing about a Bieber ringtone. Instead, it reported that the man's phone had a setting that caused it to speak the current time, and that's what had scared off the bear. Did you or a member of CEN staff insert the false detail about the Justin Bieber ringtone? If so, why? Was it inserted in order to make the story more commercially appealing?

2.
In XXX, CEN sold a story about an Argentinian teacher, apparently named Lucita Sandoval, who was alleged to have featured in a sex tape showing her having sex with a 16-year-old pupil. This story was widely picked up in Britain. The <http://www.mirror.co.uk/news/world-news/teacher-suspended-after-sex-session-4559316> Daily Mirror and <http://metro.co.uk/2014/11/03/boy-16-secretly-films-sex-with-teacher-then-uploads-it-to-whatsapp-4933699/> Metro, the Daily Mail, the <http://www.nydailynews.com/news/crime/teacher-suspended-sex-video-student-posted-whatsapp-article-1.1997562> New York Daily News and others paired it with an image of the woman posing poolside in her bikini which was credited to CEN. But two weeks before this story was sold to English language news sites, it <http://www.buzzfeed.com/ryanhatesthis/the-lucita-sandoval-sex-tape> had already been debunked by a local paper in Argentina, Nuevo Diario. As BuzzFeed News <http://www.buzzfeed.com/ryanhatesthis/the-lucita-sandoval-sex-tape#.mo4oaXjGgG> reported at the time, the video didn't show an underage boy; the woman in the video was a teacher, but she wasn't from Santiago

CONFIDENTIAL

From: Heidi Blake [heidi.blake@buzzfeed.com]
Sent: 4/1/2015 2:01:42 PM
To: Robert Colvile [robert.colvile@buzzfeed.com]
CC: Alan White [alan.white@buzzfeed.com]
Subject: Re: thoughts...

Hi both, following quick phonecall with Rob, here's my suggested revision of the email to Mike. Give me a shout if any Qs and see you tomorrow!

Dear Michael,

Thanks so much for your time this morning — I really enjoyed chatting to you and would be really pleased to continue our conversation. The idea behind our piece is to explore the challenges of reporting in the digital age in depth, and how the appetite for quick-fire viral news can end up starving serious journalism of oxygen. I'm particularly interested in the way you manage that mix, because our chat made it clear to me that your agencies are doing important, challenging investigative journalism while at the same time producing a very high volume of lighter viral or tabloid stories. I'm so interested in how you that balance works, and I'd love to talk to you about it some more. I was especially struck by your mention of your lengthy investigation into child trafficking and your failure so far to secure funding for it, and also the mention you made of women's rights in Turkey and child abuse in China — these are exactly the things that the current online ecosystem seems to make it harder and less rewarding to do. CEN seems to be a really interesting example of taking quirky stories from across the world and turning them around quickly for a western audience, and then using the proceeds (as you say) to fund more substantial investigations. I'm also interested in whether it's possible — or achievable — to bring the same kind of rigour to reporting viral stories as you would to a more traditional piece. I've noticed that some of the CEN stories which have appeared in widely in the UK media, for example this one (hyperlink) about an Argentinian teacher taped having sex with a pupil or this one (hyperlink) about a bear who was scared off by a Justin Bieber ringtone, have ended up being debunked elsewhere. Does this sort of thing end up happen because of the pressure to churn out huge amounts of quirky content to support the serious work that is clearly your big passion? In short — I think you're in a really interesting position in the current media landscape, straddling a divide between the most and least weighty forms of your trade, and I'd love a chance to chat to you about all this in depth. I would be so delighted to head over to Vienna and talk about this over lunch or a drink if you could make a bit of time to see me, or to chat to you again on the phone and talk in some more depth.

Heidi Blake

Investigations Editor

BuzzFeed UK

40 Argyll Street,

London, W1F 7EB

07481 802 294

0203 837 6042

From: Robert Colvile [robert.colvile@buzzfeed.com]
Sent: 4/24/2015 2:26:53 PM
To: roy.greenslade@mac.com
Subject: BuzzFeed story

Hi Roy,

We've never met, but we're publishing a BuzzFeed story that might interest you as an industry observer - it's an investigation of the site that provides much of the too-good-to-be-true content on the web:

http://www.buzzfeed.com/alanwhite/central-european-news

Press Gazette did a spoiler story based on briefing from the agency concerned but I think our reporting holds up. Am happy to talk you through if you're at all interested? My mobile's 07770 382438.

Best,

Robert

--

Robert Colvile | News Director

BuzzFeed: The Social News and Entertainment Company

40 Argyll Street, London, W1F 7EB

<https://lh4.googleusercontent.com/BXhoIR1nmMza8F6jkmBxHSx6UU88z_2OULVJX0wmr4WnZI8lCeky4y4QGZa-y9V3BSD5SiB6GGZNq7uG8TXOTFA7cNjtDcfnh2UMXQaHSsQLYmOi3MjCCRahWErFEJGJQg>

From: Robert Colvile [robert.colvile@buzzfeed.com]
Sent: 4/24/2015 2:26:53 PM
To: roy.greenslade@mac.com
Subject: BuzzFeed story

Hi Roy,

We've never met, but we're publishing a BuzzFeed story that might interest you as an industry observer - it's an investigation of the site that provides much of the too-good-to-be-true content on the web:

http://www.buzzfeed.com/alanwhite/central-european-news

Press Gazette did a spoiler story based on briefing from the agency concerned but I think our reporting holds up. Am happy to talk you through if you're at all interested? My mobile's 07770 382438.

Best,

Robert

--

Robert Colvile | News Director

BuzzFeed: The Social News and Entertainment Company

40 Argyll Street, London, W1F 7EB

<https://lh4.googleusercontent.com/BXhoIR1nmMza8F6jkmBxHSx6UU88z_2OULVJXOwmr4WnZI8lCeky4y4QGZay9V3BSD5SiB6GGZNq7uG8TXOTFA7cNjtDcfnh2UMXQaHSsQLYmOi3MjCCRahWErFEJGJQg>

From:	Nicolas Mora <nicolas.mora@buzzfeed.com>
To:	Conz Preti <conz.preti@buzzfeed.com>
CC:	LGBT <lgbt@buzzfeed.com>
Sent:	4/24/2015 7:43:28 PM
Subject:	Re: Transgender woman stripped, shaved and 'pulverized' by police sparking outrage	Daily Mail Online

So the pics come from CEN, which we just totally debunked and disavowed as a source. Just FYI.

On Apr 24, 2015 7:39 PM, "Conz Preti" wrote:

Everyone's talking about this in BR, maybe not worth covering right now but wanted to flag

http://www.dailymail.co.uk/news/article-3054222/Images-transgender-prisoner-face-pulverized-police-stripped-shaved-head-spark-outrage-Brazil.html?ito=social-facebook

Sent from my little phone

CONFIDENTIAL

BuzzFeed_00942

From:	Ben Smith [ben@buzzfeed.com]
Sent:	3/25/2015 8:46:58 AM
To:	Robert Colvile [robert.colvile@buzzfeed.com]
Subject:	are tom and alan close on that cen story?

Ben Smith
@buzzfeedben
cell: 646 369 3687

From: Ben Smith [ben@buzzfeed.com]
Sent: 4/14/2015 9:18:38 AM
To: Tom Phillips [tom.phillips@buzzfeed.com]
CC: Heidi Blake [heidi.blake@buzzfeed.com]
Subject: Re: We close on that cen story?

Great.

Ben Smith
@buzzfeedben
cell: 646 369 3687

On Tue, Apr 14, 2015 at 9:18 AM, Tom Phillips <tom.phillips@buzzfeed.com> wrote:

There's a No Surprises letter planned to go out tomorrow, I believe; then it's just giving him time to respond.

On Tue, Apr 14, 2015 at 1:40 PM, Ben Smith <ben@buzzfeed.com> wrote:

--

Ben Smith
@buzzfeedben
cell: 646 369 3687 <tel:646%20369%203687>

--

Tom Phillips | Editorial Director, BuzzFeed UK

07773 914795 | @flashboy

BuzzFeed

2nd Floor, 40 Argyll Street

London, W1F 7EB

<https://lh4.googleusercontent.com/o9_nWc4WcPZ1PbEHnX7yKFasrpr2G2CqQD6kK2W6JXdzDa40mOjP1IG6dY6dCmDbv9kZcitAGPciMjo4diXCy3i8lt3302Y67u6loCoFSMJSUd74tv03GAdZeUEQPODF_w>

From:	Alan White <alan.white@buzzfeed.com>
To:	Heidi Blake <heidi.blake@buzzfeed.com>
CC:	Mark Schoofs <mark.schoofs@buzzfeed.com>;Tom Phillips <tom.phillips@buzzfeed.com>
Sent:	3/31/2015 7:29:16 AM
Subject:	Re: Would you two have 10 mins to chat with Tom and I today?

Great, just give us a shout, we'll clear schedule

On Tue, Mar 31, 2015 at 12:28 PM, Heidi Blake wrote:

We're interviewing until about 2.30 and from 6 but we'll be back in the office for a couple of hours this afternoon so let's catch up then?

Heidi Blake

Investigations Editor

BuzzFeed UK

40 Argyll Street,

London, W1F 7EB

07481 802 294

0203 837 6042

@HeidiIBlake

On Tue, Mar 31, 2015 at 10:45 AM, Alan White wrote:

Just wanting a bit of advice on CEN stuff....

From:	Alan White
To:	Luke Lewis
CC:	Tom Phillips; Craig Silverman; Heidi Blake
Sent:	4/12/2015 11:06:58 AM
Subject:	Re: No surprises letter

Purely personal safety. We're telling him we're about to destroy a business that took him over a decade to build along with his entire professional credibility. You just do not know how a person will react to being put in that situation, nor who he knows out there. If that sounds over cautious so be it, I've ended up in a bad situation before when I thought there was no risk at all.

On 12 Apr 2015, at 15:07, Luke Lewis <&lta href="mailto:luke.lewis@buzzfeed.com">luke.lewis@buzzfeed.com

Thanks Alan, letter looks solid to me. What are the arguments against going to speak to him in person?

On 12 Apr 2015 1:01 pm, "Alan White" <&lta href="mailto:alan.white@buzzfeed.com">alan.white@buzzfeed.com

Hello all,

Front up letter below.

- So Craig, Tom, Heidi - above all, have I missed anything from the piece here which could be alleged to be defamatory? What else do I need to put to him?

- Reminder that Schoofs advises it's sent in multiple ways - email, courier, physical letter etc. Let's get that side of things organised. As we're doing this, I've not hyperlinked to stories in this email.

Leidig will then be given five days to reply. In that time we need to be:

- Double checking that we have screenshotted EVERYTHING pertaining to this story. EVERYTHING. Because if alarms go off at Daily Mail/Mirror etc once he gets this communication, they could try to start updating/amending. Which in itself is a story. Tom - can you double check? Go through line by line etc. Have we got the charity form for e.g.?
- I want to lead with Lucita Sandoval rather than Bieber bear. Is there anything we can do to make this happen?
- Approaching the Mirror and the Mail press offices. Who else?
- Talk to BuzzFeed News reporters about updating their posts.

CONFIDENTIAL

From:	Ben Smith
To:	Shani Hilton
CC:	Lisa Tozzi; Robert Colvile; Nabiha Syed; Tom Namako; Luke Lewis; Heidi Blake; Craig Silverman; Craig Silverman; Alan White; Tom Phillips; Mark Stephens, CBE; Allison Lucas; Matthew Tucker; Rory Lewarne
Sent:	4/24/2015 2:18:15 PM
Subject:	Re: CEN - hopefully final copy

Awesome.

On Friday, April 24, 2015, Shani Hilton <&lta href="mailto:shani.hilton@buzzfeed.com">shani.hilton@buzzfeed.com
hurrah! now you can go to the pub :)

On Fri, Apr 24, 2015 at 2:14 PM, Lisa Tozzi <&lta href="javascript:_e(%7B%7D,'cvml','lisa.tozzi@buzzfeed.com');" target="_blank">lisa.tozzi@buzzfeed.com wrote:
Congratulations. Looking forward to reading!

On Fri, Apr 24, 2015 at 2:11 PM, Robert Colvile <&lta href="javascript:_e(%7B%7D,'cvml','robert.colvile@buzzfeed.com');" target="_blank">robert.colvile@buzzfeed.com wrote:
PUBBED!

http://www.buzzfeed.com/alanwhite/central-european-news

Thank you all for your patience. We're tidying up at this end but it's now live.

On 24 April 2015 at 16:31, Nabiha Syed <&lta href="javascript:_e(%7B%7D,'cvml','nabiha.syed@buzzfeed.com');" target="_blank">nabiha.syed@buzzfeed.com wrote:

Nabiha Syed | Assistant General Counsel
BuzzFeed
200 Fifth Avenue, 8th Floor, NY, NY 10010
(646) 660-9617 (w) | (714) 200-3983 (c)
nabiha.syed@buzzfeed.com
PGP: AD1C 49CD A5B8 2B7A 9AB1 6E40 A807 3732 BCA1 1DEE

On Fri, Apr 24, 2015 at 8:19 AM, Ben Smith <&lta href="javascript:_e(%7B%7D,'cvml','ben@buzzfeed.com');" target="_blank">ben@buzzfeed.com wrote:

On Friday, April 24, 2015, Robert Colvile <&lta href="javascript:_e(%7B%7D,'cvml','robert.colvile@buzzfeed.com');" target="_blank">robert.colvile@buzzfeed.com
For info, the Press Gazette piece is now live.

http://www.pressgazette.co.uk/buzzfeed-investigation-emails-harm-business-competitor-online-news-provider

On 24 April 2015 at 16:14, Robert Colvile <&lta>robert.colvile@buzzfeed.com wrote:
Hi everyone,

From:	Robert Colvile <robert.colvile@buzzfeed.com>
To:	Alan White <alan.white@buzzfeed.com>
Sent:	4/24/2015 11:45:36 AM
Subject:	Re: CEN - hopefully final copy

Sure

On 24 April 2015 at 16:42, Alan White wrote:

Am happy.

One thought - Additional reporting: Tanya Chen. (She looked into knickers story for us)

On 24 Apr 2015, at 16:14, Robert Colvile wrote:

--

Robert Colvile | News Director

BuzzFeed: The Social News and Entertainment Company

40 Argyll Street, London, W1F 7EB

--

CONFIDENTIAL

BuzzFeed_01136

From:	Alan White <alan.white@buzzfeed.com>
To:	Robert Colvile <robert.colvile@buzzfeed.com>
CC:	Craig Silverman <craig.silverman@buzzfeed.com>;Tom Phillips <tom.phillips@buzzfeed.com>
Sent:	4/24/2015 10:39:58 AM
Subject:	Re: Final CEN copy

On my phone and can't find it.

Here's a substitute if no one else on it - will need a different wording for link
http://m.huffpost.com/us/entry/5508138

It's on this page I think but can't scroll down on mobile
http://touch.metro.se/tema/viralgranskaren/

On 24 Apr 2015, at 15:14, Robert Colvile wrote:

Just flagged up to Tom - the link isn't working to the Viral Examiner debunking of the half-naked sunbather... links to the original stories work fine though. Can someone send over while I plough through?

On 24 April 2015 at 15:01, Robert Colvile wrote:

Great, thanks.

On 24 April 2015 at 14:43, Craig Silverman wrote:

FYI about a small item in the grand scheme of things: it looks like the story will go live after it's public that I'm on staff. So you may want to add in the line now that says I recently joined BuzzFeed full-time (though this work predated that). I will be getting the folks in NY to change my byline from Contributor to Canada editor, or something to that effect. So it will show up that way when we publish. I'm fully online and available if you need anything else from me.

On Fri, Apr 24, 2015 at 9:37 AM, Robert Colvile wrote:

On 24 April 2015 at 14:36, Luke Lewis wrote:

On Fri, Apr 24, 2015 at 2:02 PM, Matthew Tucker wrote:

CONFIDENTIAL

From:	Craig Silverman
To:	Alan White
CC:	Tom Phillips
Sent:	1/19/2015 12:41:16 PM
Subject:	Re: CEN ad!

Looking good. Only other note I'd make on the ones you've added is that you haven't done the truthiness rating for them. (You click on each link you added and in the left hand column you can enter how that article talks about the claim.) We'll have to do those ratings in order to get the pages to show the stats and share counts. But not essential to do it now.

I agree that a Chinese speaker seems to be important. So many recent claims come from there.

On 19 January 2015 at 09:27, Alan White <&lta href="mailto:alan.white@buzzfeed.com" target="_blank">alan.white@buzzfeed.com wrote:
I think it's absolutely worth chucking in an application. Would love to hear from him how this "virtual news team "works.

Today I've taken 9 stories, tidied up four that are debunked or (in the case of the cat) verified to some degree and then had a look at five where we can't work out what's going on to see if I can get more of a handle on their methods. All those got added to Emergent, Craig you might like to check I've done it right.

I feel like if I want to progress these I need someone who can speak Chinese and has some experience with Weibo, and some time. I've got access to the native Chinese speakers at BuzzFeed list, so I can ping out some emails to them tomorrow. There are a couple of other ideas for verifying which I can try too.

Let me know your thoughts....

On Mon, Jan 19, 2015 at 3:54 PM, Craig Silverman <&lta href="mailto:silvermancraig@gmail.com" target="_blank">silvermancraig@gmail.com wrote:
Pretty incredible. Over the years Leidig has written pieces for the Press Gazette and also gotten coverage from them. This may be one of the better ways to actually get on the phone with him...

On 19 January 2015 at 07:36, Tom Phillips <&lta href="mailto:tom.phillips@buzzfeed.com" target="_blank">tom.phillips@buzzfeed.com wrote:
Oh wow. I think... do we need someone to apply for this job?

On Mon, Jan 19, 2015 at 3:33 PM, Alan White <&lta href="mailto:alan.white@buzzfeed.com" target="_blank">alan.white@buzzfeed.com wrote:
http://www.pressgazette.co.uk/senior-reporter-sought-central-european-news-home-based

--
Alan White
Breaking News Reporter, BuzzFeed UK
@_aljwhite

19-21 Hatton Garden
London EC1N 8BA

From:	Craig Silverman [silvermancraig@gmail.com]
Sent:	3/28/2015 5:02:23 PM
To:	Alan White [alan.white@buzzfeed.com]
Subject:	Re: CEN stories text/photos proof - Invitation to edit

One other note re: the Leidig approach. I totally agree with what Heidi suggested and you said in terms of being friendly up front.

One thing to keep in mind is that he clearly has a high opinion of the real journalism he does. You can cite his Bernie Madoff book and the stuff he has written for Press Gazette to say that he is clearly a serious journo and ask him about how he has seen things evolve with the advent of online news. I think he would love to see himself quoted as an authority of how the web has changed content economics and how it has hurt original reporting. That does seem like the best way to get him to agree to talk. Also, the fact that you guys previously bought from him may help him open up at first.

I'm in my way to the airport and will work more won the text tonight and Monday. Expect to see some revisions by Monday morning your time.

Craig

On Saturday, March 28, 2015, Craig Silverman <silvermancraig@gmail.com> wrote:
Good to hear re: the tapeworm. The only tricky thing right now is that we lead with the Argentinian one and that does not show up on their sites. So if we have any way to confirm via other sources that they sold text and photos, that would really help us for the lead. Otherwise we may need to swap it out for either Bieber or the recent naked Russian debunk.

Also, if we're reaching out to folks to check for CEN copy, let's also ask them about the hoax story about the Chinese woman looking for strangers to fund her travel. As of now we have a Telegraph story with a CEN photo credit but no story on other sites. However, they did publish a debunk of it: http://austriantimes.at/news/Around_the_World/2014-10-29/51901/China_Closes_30_Million_User_App_For_Faking_Sex_Advert-newentry So it would be great to show that they sold the hoax and then published the debunk.

On 28 March 2015 at 05:19, Alan White <alan.white@buzzfeed.com> wrote:
Cheers Craig.

FYI Tapeworm story's fine - we definitely bought the copy. I don't know if we still have those emails (I don't, our picture ed possibly does).

Our legal team are working through now. Quite plausible I'll be in a position to reach out to him on Monday. Will contact you on plan of attack first, but personally I'm all for the tread softly, then gradually amp up the questions, approach.

Alan

On Fri, Mar 27, 2015 at 8:44 PM, Craig Silverman (via Google Sheets) <silvermancraig@gmail.com> wrote:
Craig Silverman has invited you to edit the following spreadsheet:

From:	Alan White [alan.white@buzzfeed.com]
Sent:	4/3/2015 5:13:43 AM
To:	Craig Silverman [silvermancraig@gmail.com]
CC:	Tom Phillips [tom.phillips@buzzfeed.com]
Subject:	Re: CEN Final - Invitation to edit

Great. Heidi's advised us to keep all email contact to a minimum from this point on in case we have to disclose it in court as it can be twisted out of context, but will set up a call when there's a significant development. Am pushing for face-to-face meeting.

On Fri, Apr 3, 2015 at 2:58 AM, Craig Silverman <silvermancraig@gmail.com> wrote:
Thanks, and sorry for the delayed reply. I had a nightmare of a trip back from Hamburg that involved 23 hours of consecutive travel. Great that you got a chance to at least chat with him. Keep me posted on whether he replies and if I can help with anything else.

Craig

On 1 April 2015 at 12:59, Alan White <alan.white@buzzfeed.com> wrote:
G chatted you an update re Leidig Craig.

Next email to him being sent tomorrow morning.

On Mon, Mar 30, 2015 at 5:51 PM, Alan White <alan.white@buzzfeed.com> wrote:
Great, cheers.

Nothing from Leidig yet. We'll discuss next stages with Schoofs / Heidi tomorrow, but let's contemplate the possibility of a no surprises letter.

On Mon, Mar 30, 2015 at 5:50 PM, Tom Phillips <tom.phillips@buzzfeed.com> wrote:
Yes, I should have time.

On Mon, Mar 30, 2015 at 5:47 PM, Alan White <alan.white@buzzfeed.com> wrote:
Tom, would you have any time tomorrow to screenshot the webpages? I might.

On Mon, Mar 30, 2015 at 10:27 AM, Craig Silverman (via Google Docs) <silvermancraig@gmail.com> wrote:
Craig Silverman has invited you to edit the following document:

CEN Final

Hi guys,

Here is a new draft. I'll send along an email with more info.

Craig

Open in Docs

CONFIDENTIAL

From: Craig Silverman <silvermancraig@gmail.com>
To: Tom Phillips <tom.phillips@buzzfeed.com>
CC: Alan White <alan.white@buzzfeed.com>
Sent: 12/31/2014 10:33:39 AM
Subject: Re: Verification, CEN and Emergent

Hi guys,

Happy new year and other holiday greetings! I hope you've had some time off. I've finished off a few projects and am ready to start more digging on this if you're still game. I just added myself to seven of the 22 stories we have in the spreadsheet. My thought was we would divide the work in three, but I'm happy to take on more if you like. Just let me know. The other bit of new is that we made some updates to Emergent that would enable us to capture the social share counts for each of these stories (and all the articles about them).

So we could create a claim page for each of these and enter in all the URL's we find, as well as the information we gather about them. This can stay private until we are ready to publish. When that happens, we can add a tag to each of them which then makes it easy to have them all on one page for comparison or linking to. Here's an example of a claim page generated by the ISSI tag:

http://www.emergent.info/tag/ISIS

We can also back date them so that they don't show up as new on the Emergent homepage (seeing as they are old stories.) This may all sound unclear as it's easier if I just show you what the backend looks like. I'd be happy to do that Friday if you're in the office, or next week can also work.

Tom, I'll also email you to work out the working relationship.

Best regards,
Craig

On 3 December 2014 at 17:02, Craig Silverman wrote:

I just found another one:
http://austriantimes.at/image/40313/news/Around_the_World/2014-12-03/52021/Ski_Resort_Opens_With_Snow_Stored_From_Last_Season

They wrote it up like its new, but the main pic and associated story appear to be four years old:
http://www.oe24.at/oesterreich/chronik/salzburg/Saalbach-lagerte-das-weisse-Gold/5736774

The other two pics get nothing on a reverse image search, though. It's possible this happens every year, so I will check on that. Just about to take off so I will add this to the doc later.

Craig

On 3 December 2014 at 12:47, Craig Silverman wrote:

Yes, let's grab stories each to dig into on separate pages. Tracking the spread and shares is something Emergent is built to do really well. the only hitch is we are looking at old stories for the most part, and any new claims I publish to the site are automatically listed at the top. Let me check with my dev to see if we can backdate publishing. That way we'd have a database to just load URLs into and the shares get calculated automatically. We could then do a CSV export to compare who runs their stuff the most.

On 3 December 2014 at 12:39, Tom Phillips wrote:

OK, I'm going to look at some of the ones you've added to the doc, and I'm also going to start going through some old stories I did from their copy at Metro years ago, just to see if I can trace some patterns back.

Shall we just divide up the doc into pages for seperate stories, put our names down for any as-yet-undebunked ones we are going to look at, and add in results of any reearch in as we go? That way we've got a sort of breadcrumb trail of our research.

Additionally, Alan suggests having a spreadsheet where we can list all the sites that ran each particular story – I've set up the very rudimentary beginning stages of one here .

On Wed, Dec 3, 2014 at 5:19 PM, Craig Silverman wrote:

Hi guys,

I'm looking forward to working together on this. I just loaded in a bunch of suspect stories, two of which are of the penis-chopping variety. The others originated on Leidig's Croatian Times and Austrian Times sites. They have suspect sourcing and pics. Looks like we have a lot to go through and I'd say that Tom's suspicion that trouble starts when they go far afield form Eastern Europe is correct.

How do we want to divide up the work? And we should think also think about our methodology for looking into these. That way we can say we applied the same test for each of them.

Best regards,
Craig

On 2 December 2014 at 09:34, Alan White wrote:

Google hangout here

https://plus.google.com/hangouts/_/gu3zxptdjl3lklxz6lbjidut6ma

On Mon, Dec 1, 2014 at 6:53 PM, Tom Phillips wrote:

That works for me too – look forward to talking then!

On Mon, Dec 1, 2014 at 6:12 PM, Craig Silverman wrote:

Hangout is good with me.

On 1 December 2014 at 13:08, Alan White wrote:

Works for me! Tom?

What's your preferred method of communication? Google hangout?

On Mon, Dec 1, 2014 at 6:06 PM, Craig Silverman wrote:

Oh gosh -- sorry. That is a silly time to ask to talk. I for some reason had it in my mind that later afternoon was good for you. I could do 9:30 am my time tomorrow morning if that's more sane.

On 1 December 2014 at 12:17, Alan White wrote:

Hi Craig,

Lovely to meet you too. It would be great to do a definitive piece on CEN. Surprised one hasn't already been done to be honest. So this would be 9pm GMT. I could make that - Tom?

On Mon, Dec 1, 2014 at 4:03 PM, Craig Silverman wrote:

Hey guys,

Alan, very nice to meet you! Tom, thanks for the intro. I have a couple of other CEN stories that I would add to the list. I am trying to dig into one right now, though I am committed to doing that for Digg. (We have a content partnership whereby I write up some of the rumors I track for them as Digg Originals.)

I'd love to talk, as I think CEN needs to be exposed. I'd also love to chat about Emergent in general. I'm currently working to raise financing for it and am also looking for partnerships, such as the initial one I have with Digg. I'm heading to the middle east on Wednesday but I could talk today at 4 pm Montreal time (same time zone as New York) or tomorrow at 5 pm.

Best regards,
Craig

On 1 December 2014 at 10:50, Tom Phillips wrote:

Hey Craig – just wanted to drop you a line for a couple of reasons...

First up, I just wanted to introduce you a chap on our news team here at BuzzFeed UK - Alan White. Alan's one of our resident viral news experts and is very good at spotting hoaxes from a mile off, so he'd a handy guy to know. Alan, meet Craig. Craig and I go way back (in internet debunking years).

Secondly, we've been thinking about doing a piece on CEN/Central European News as a source for a large number of dubious stories that go big on the web (such as the Justin Bieber/bear story you wrote about – I remember we've chatted about them before.) A lot of their stuff falls into that tricky territory of "looks unlikely but hard to definitively

From:	Tom Phillips <tom.phillips@buzzfeed.com>
To:	Alan White <alan.white@buzzfeed.com>
CC:	Luke Lewis <luke.lewis@buzzfeed.com>;Richard James <richard.james@buzzfeed.com>
Sent:	12/2/2014 12:52:21 PM
Subject:	Re: CEN story

Yes I will liaise.

On Tue, Dec 2, 2014 at 5:50 PM, Alan White wrote:

Happy to aim for December 19.

Will try to do a bit of work over the weekend and get the full list of debunked and debunkable stuff together.

Tom are you ok to do all the liaising with Craig?

On Tue, Dec 2, 2014 at 5:40 PM, Luke Lewis wrote:

I don't know, Christmas is not a complete dead zone. People still go on the internet and read things.

On Tue, Dec 2, 2014 at 5:37 PM, Tom Phillips wrote:

Let the three of us have a look at what material we've got already before we put a specific deadline on it. We'll revisit in a day or two and see if we're looking at a couple of weeks' turnaround, or if we should set a deadline in January instead (no point publishing over Christmas, I suspect.)

On Tue, Dec 2, 2014 at 5:33 PM, Luke Lewis wrote:

We should put a deadline on it though, otherwise it'll never happen. Publish by December 19?

On Tue, Dec 2, 2014 at 5:32 PM, Richard James wrote:

But what you guys have lined up sounds bang on and has potential to be really incredible.

Richard James | News Editor UK | @richjamesuk

BuzzFeed: The Social News and Entertainment Company

19-21 Hatton Garden, London, EC1N 8BA

On Tue, Dec 2, 2014 at 5:31 PM, Richard James wrote:

We aren't immune to publishing fake news/falling for hoaxes ourselves, so as long as we focus on the incredible pick-up this guy's ridiculous stories get across the world we're on firmer footing than simply screen grabbing 10 Mail stories.

Could tie in the fact second/third sourcing, getting unique quotes, is disappearing from news room as they simple turn to churning out as many stories (no matter how improbable) as possible.

Richard James | News Editor UK | @richjamesuk

BuzzFeed: The Social News and Entertainment Company

19-21 Hatton Garden, London, EC1N 8BA

On Tue, Dec 2, 2014 at 5:27 PM, Luke Lewis wrote:

All sounds good, as you say we should not take an aggressive or holier than thou tone.

I like the idea of styling CEN as a "viral bullshit factory", but "king of viral hoaxes" may be better. We'll see.

Can't wait to read it.

On Tue, Dec 2, 2014 at 5:14 PM, Alan White wrote:

Errr just that we might need to substitute "Bullshit" for something a little milder. Or maybe not.

I think we're treading a real tightrope with this piece. Because the truth is that however much we hedge it we will be saying "Look at the shit Metro / Mirror / Mail run as truth and that we don't." Which is fine, it's just that as Tom says it needs to be sensitive - it's a wider look at how the whole process of news production has changed, not a straight up hit job on him and the people buying the stories. Well, not quite.

On Tue, Dec 2, 2014 at 5:08 PM, Tom Phillips wrote:

Hey chaps – so Alan and I had a good hangout with Craig Silverman this afternoon, talking about CEN and fake news. We're keen to collaborate with him (and he wants to work with us) on a long-ish piece about CEN – he's already got a lot of research on some of their stories, and on the organisation/bloke behind it. It sounds to us a lot like it's not just a news agency that sells dubious stories, the guy may be quite odd/dodgy in many ways.

We're keen that it shouldn't look like we're running a hit piece on our competitors for publishing CEN stories, so we're going to try and focus it more on the debunking, the agency itself, and a general --thinkpiece-- take on the production of viral news. (And acknowledge that we personally have both run CEN pieces in the past.)

Working title, thanks to Alan, is "How One Man In Austria Became The King Of Viral Bullshit".

Thoughts/questions?

--

Tom Phillips
Senior Writer, BuzzFeed UK

19-21 Hatton Garden
London, EC1N 8BA
07773914795 | @flashboy

--

Alan White
Breaking News Reporter, BuzzFeed UK

@aljwhite

19-21 Hatton Garden
London EC1N 8BA

--

Luke Lewis | Editor-in-Chief, BuzzFeed UK | 07967 215436 | @lukelewis

BuzzFeed: The Social News and Entertainment Company

21 Hatton Garden, London, EC1N 8BA

From: Tom Phillips <tom.phillips@buzzfeed.com>
To: Alan White <alan.white@buzzfeed.com>
Sent: 3/23/2015 6:56:06 PM
Subject: Re: cen

my fave note there btw is "[BORING CUT ALL OF THIS.]"

On Mon, Mar 23, 2015 at 10:52 PM, Tom Phillips wrote:

Agreed. TBH I think that might be when we drop the bulk of the "BuzzFeed did some of this" material (and tbh not just that – I have to acknowledge that I used them in a previous job, etc.)

Think I've fucked up track changes but here's where I am with my pass on it (not all the way through). Mostly just tried to make it punchier.

On Mon, Mar 23, 2015 at 10:45 PM, Alan White wrote:

Yes indeed.

Was also thinking, one thing worth putting in towards the end is maybe some grandiose thoughts on what this actually says about modern media. i.e., what does it tell us that the Telegraph and Indy have been reduced to reproducing this nonsense?

I mean, we get that those brands aren't what they were and are chasing clicks like everyone else, but would a proper old school news editor ever let people touch this stuff?

We've done 6,000 words, may as well not piss about and go full pretentious.

On 23 Mar 2015, at 22:01, Tom Phillips wrote:

btw just pinged miriam elder to ask if she'd ever had a run-in with CEN – never heard of them. she suggested I ask Max, which I have now done, waiting for a response.

(obvs it now occurs to me that if loads of experienced correspondents in eastern europe have never heard of them that's almost as lol as them having heard of them)

--

Tom Phillips | Editorial Director, BuzzFeed UK

07773 914795 | @flashboy

BuzzFeed

From: Heidi Blake [heidi.blake@buzzfeed.com]
Sent: 3/25/2015 4:17:51 PM
To: Alan White [alan.white@buzzfeed.com]
CC: Robert Colvile [robert.colvile@buzzfeed.com]
Subject: Re: Touching base

Sure thing

Heidi Blake | UK Investigations Editor

BuzzFeed News

40 Argyll Street,

London, W1F 7EB

@HeidiIBlake <https://twitter.com/HeidiIBlake>

On Wed, Mar 25, 2015 at 8:09 PM, Alan White <alan.white@buzzfeed.com> wrote:

Hoo boy. You see, I feel the tenor of this piece is going to change once we approach him. Understand I can't show to Craig, but do you mind me sending to Tom? He's going to be co-bylined.

On Wed, Mar 25, 2015 at 7:57 PM, Heidi Blake <heidi.blake@buzzfeed.com> wrote:

In confidence, dug out this email from Leidig ... We spoke last year about a big investigation he was doing into child trafficking and he got in touch on LinkedIn to see if it might work for BuzzFeed & followed up by email. Interesting that he leapt to defend the 'tabloid' stories they do without me even asking about them – and says that they churn those out to drum up funding for their investigations. I never got round to responding to this but in light of your stuff it's quite interesting ...

Heidi Blake | UK Investigations Editor

BuzzFeed News

40 Argyll Street,

London, W1F 7EB

@HeidiIBlake <https://twitter.com/HeidiIBlake>

---------- Forwarded message ----------
From: Michael Leidig <editor@cen.at>

From: Heidi Blake [heidi.blake@buzzfeed.com]
Sent: 3/31/2015 10:38:24 AM
To: Alan White [alan.white@buzzfeed.com]
Subject: Mike Leidig's contact details

CEN Ltd.
Hadikgasse 96
A-1140 Vienna
Austria
Telephone: ~~+43 1 812 128 719~~
24-hr news m~~obile:~~ 57465

Michael Leid~~ig~~

Michael Leidig <michaelleidig@me.com>

Heidi Blake

Investigations Editor

BuzzFeed UK

40 Argyll Street,

London, W1F 7EB

07481 802 294

0203 837 6042

<https://twitter.com/HeidilBlake> @HeidilBlake

From:	Alan White [alan.white@buzzfeed.com]
Sent:	4/21/2015 6:55:38 AM
To:	Sean Walsh [sean.walsh@mailonline.com]
CC:	Editorial Dailymailonline [editorial@mailonline.co.uk]; Ted Young [ted.young@metro.co.uk]
Subject:	Re: Story about Metro / MailOnline

Cheers Sean.

I believe there are 10 other publications mentioned besides Mailonline.

On Tue, Apr 21, 2015 at 11:53 AM, Sean Walsh <Sean.Walsh@mailonline.com> wrote:

Hi Alan - a quick note to acknowledge receipt of your email. We will come back to you.

Are we the only publication mentioned in the piece or will you be including other publications who license CEN's copy?

Regards
Sean

Sean Walsh
Director of Communications & Media Relations,   <http://DailyMail.com> DailyMail.com
+1-646-678-2858 <tel:%2B1-646-678-2858>

On Apr 21, 2015, at 6:38 AM, "Alan White" <alan.white@buzzfeed.com> wrote:

Dear Sirs,

BuzzFeed News is preparing to publish an article in which we will report that two Daily Mail Group news outlets - MailOnline and Metro - have bought stories from the news agency CEN that have subsequently been proven false either in part or in their entirety, or contain quotes of questionable provenance. We would be really grateful if you could send us your response to this by 5pm Wednesday April 22 so we can make sure we include it in our report.

Here are the stories in question:

1. In August 2014, MailOnline ran a story about a man who was apparently saved from a bear attack by a Justin Bieber ringtone on his phone ("Russian fisherman saved from bear attack when ringtone featuring one of the pop brat's songs scares it away", MailOnline, 5 August 2014). However, the original story about the bear attack, <http://www.kp.ru/daily/26263.4/3141355/> which was published in Russia's Komsomolskaya Pravda, said nothing about a Bieber ringtone. Instead, it reported that the man's phone had a setting that caused it to speak the current time, and that's what had scared off the bear. Is MailOnline aware that this story is fake? Did MailOnline look into the story at all after it had purchased the copy?

2. In a <http://www.dailymail.co.uk/news/article-2947440/Thief-25-tricked-elderly-women-thinking-lost-little-boy-wearing-nappy-sucking-lollipop-let-homes-Paraguay.html> story about a thief in Paraguay who apparently broke into people's homes by pretending to be a baby ("Thief, 25, tricked elderly women into thinking he was a lost little boy by wearing a nappy and sucking a lollipop so they would let him into their homes in Paraguay", MailOnline, 10 February 2015), there are quotes from a local, Lara Orta Ornelas, 59, who said:

"I am surprised that the police have only just now arrested him. He has been doing this for years and I know the police have had complaints before but it's incredible that they never realised the baby is actually a fully grown man."

CONFIDENTIAL

From: Craig Silverman [silvermancraig@gmail.com]
Sent: 1/16/2015 1:56:55 PM
To: Alan White [alan.white@buzzfeed.com]
Subject: Re: Emergent instructions

Sounds good. I will do some today and early next week as well.

On 16 January 2015 at 13:55, Alan White <alan.white@buzzfeed.com> wrote:

No problem. My plan for Monday/Tue is just to upload as many as I can, also pick off as many of the low hanging fruit that I can verify/debunk online, and then Tom will probably step in Wed/Thur and we can see where we are by the end of the week.

On Fri, Jan 16, 2015 at 6:53 PM, Craig Silverman <silvermancraig@gmail.com> wrote:

Oh wait. I just tried to relogin and got an error message. We just pushed a bunch of changes and it may have broken something. Let me get someone to look at it.

On 16 January 2015 at 13:51, Craig Silverman <silvermancraig@gmail.com> wrote:

No prob! You should get a prompt to login when you go to http://www.edit.emergent.info. The screen you should see is attached. But if that doesn't come up, maybe try this:

https://edit.emergent.info/login

On 16 January 2015 at 13:48, Alan White <alan.white@buzzfeed.com> wrote:

ludicrously stupid question #1

I can't find the login button!

On Fri, Jan 16, 2015 at 6:42 PM, Craig Silverman <silvermancraig@gmail.com> wrote:

Hi guys,

Here's a quick recap of the instructions for loading in claims/articles in emergent:

* Go to edit.emergent.info

* Sign in the with Gmail account you'd sent me. (Just click the Login with your Google account link.)

* Enter-a-slug-like-this that describes the story. This will be the URL.

* Enter in the core claim of the story. An example is, "Claim: A woman cut off her husband's penis twice." They are entered with the Claim: at the front and no period at the end.
* You can add info in the description that fleshes out the basic details of what allegedly happened. Optional.
* Click the Add Story button.
* Do a Find on the page for the claim you just created or scroll all the way to the bottom. It will be the last one listed. Click on the claim text to open its page.
* Chose the category and then add tags. Make sure you put in the CEN tag so we have one page with everything.
* Add in info in the Origin text box about where the story first came from and how CEN got it. Add a relevant URL if you have one.
* If you know it's true or false, choose the appropriate radio button in the upper right and then put in the info about why you know it's true or false, and add in a debunking URL if you have one. I suspect in many cases the debunking URL will be the story on BuzzFeed. That can be added in later.
* Paste in the URLs of all the places that covered the story. Click on each of them to add the Truthiness rating (meaning how the story reported the claim) for the headline and body text. Click Save Version.
* Profit.

From:	Heidi Blake [heidi.blake@buzzfeed.com]
Sent:	4/7/2015 9:19:23 AM
To:	Alan White [alan.white@buzzfeed.com]
CC:	Luke Lewis [luke.lewis@buzzfeed.com]
Subject:	Re: Can we chat today?

Hi both! My understanding was that this was going to be held till Rob was back because it's a sensitive story and needs careful handling. Very happy to talk strategy though. Any word from Leidig, Alan? If not and if you're done trying to talk to CEN staffers who he could shut down I would get a detailed front-up letter written and ready to send him. I think the more time we give him to respond the better. But let's talk in more detail tomorrow. Cheers!

Heidi Blake

Investigations Editor

BuzzFeed UK

40 Argyll Street,

London, W1F 7EB

07481 802 294

0203 837 6042

<https://twitter.com/HeidilBlake> @HeidilBlake

On Tue, Apr 7, 2015 at 9:15 AM, Alan White <alan.white@buzzfeed.com> wrote:

Yeah - no problem. Re timing/next steps personally I'm happy to defer to you, I'm happy to hold over as long as we want - Rob never said waiting for him was a plan? Just copying Luke.

On Tue, Apr 7, 2015 at 2:13 PM, Heidi Blake <heidi.blake@buzzfeed.com> wrote:

Hey Alan,

Today is really tricky for me because we have two interviewees visiting the office and I'm going to be with them all day. But I could talk tomorrow? What's the latest plan on the timing? Did you talk to Rob about holding this over till he's back from paternity?

Heidi Blake

Investigations Editor

BuzzFeed UK

40 Argyll Street,

London, W1F 7EB

CONFIDENTIAL

From:	Alan White
To:	Tanya Chen
CC:	Craig Silverman; Tom Phillips
Sent:	3/31/2015 11:19:30 AM
Subject:	Re: What Is People's Daily Online like?

Yeah, that's something to work with. Thanks Tanya!

On Tue, Mar 31, 2015 at 4:18 PM, Tanya Chen <&lta href="mailto:tanya.chen@buzzfeed.com" target="_blank">tanya.chen@buzzfeed.com wrote:
Asked around, and most people haven't heard of it. A friend of my mom's, however, has read their articles and trusts them as a news source? At least considers them "legitimate "on some level. Hope that helps!

On Mon, Mar 30, 2015 at 3:44 PM, Alan White <&lta href="mailto:alan.white@buzzfeed.com" target="_blank">alan.white@buzzfeed.com wrote:
Thanks Tanya! Yeah....sorry........

On Mon, Mar 30, 2015 at 6:58 PM, Tanya Chen <&lta href="mailto:tanya.chen@buzzfeed.com" target="_blank">tanya.chen@buzzfeed.com wrote:
Hey!

I've never heard of the site, so can't say too much, but I'll ask around to get a better sense. Will let you know!

(and my god... this story)

On Mon, Mar 30, 2015 at 9:19 AM, Alan White <&lta href="mailto:alan.white@buzzfeed.com" target="_blank">alan.white@buzzfeed.com wrote:
Hey Tanya

So since we started doing this investigation MailOnline has started linking out to a site called People's Daily Online

Warning - this one is super grim

http://www.dailymail.co.uk/news/peoplesdaily/article-3017695/Heart-breaking-moment-five-year-old-girl-finds-missing-pet-dog-Flower-sold-ready-cooked-Vietnamese-stall.html

Do you know anything about the site CEN is seemingly in partnership with? Are they reputable?

--
Alan White
Breaking News Reporter, BuzzFeed UK
@ aljwhite

2nd Floor, 40 Argyll Street,
London, W1F 7EB

--
Tanya Chen
| Senior Editor, Canada |
@tanya_chen

From:	Ben Smith <ben@buzzfeed.com>
To:	Lisa Tozzi <lisa.tozzi@buzzfeed.com>
CC:	Robert Colvile <robert.colvile@buzzfeed.com>;Tom Namako <tom.namako@buzzfeed.com>;Alan White <alan.white@buzzfeed.com>
Sent:	4/23/2015 1:20:12 PM
Subject:	Re: Central European News Ltd [CR-PCR1.FID107637]

We should upload it and link to it, as well as quoting from it. Zero obligation to them.

Ben Smith
@buzzfeedben
cell: 646 369 3687

On Thu, Apr 23, 2015 at 12:54 PM, Lisa Tozzi wrote:

On Thu, Apr 23, 2015 at 12:52 PM, Robert Colvile wrote:

Rob

On 23 April 2015 at 16:37, Robert Colvile wrote:

On 23 April 2015 at 16:35, Ben Smith wrote:

Ben Smith
@buzzfeedben
cell: 646 369 3687

On Wed, Apr 22, 2015 at 12:51 PM, Robert Colvile wrote:

We also asked for and have now received statements from the Mail and Mirror, which apparently prompted a certain level of alarm in their offices.

CONFIDENTIAL

From:	Alan White <alan.white@buzzfeed.com>
To:	Craig Silverman <silvermancraig@gmail.com>
CC:	Tom Phillips <tom.phillips@buzzfeed.com>
Sent:	1/30/2015 5:29:24 AM
Subject:	Re: Penis update

I've messaged a friend at the Mail. She's going to try and think of someone on the pic desk she can trust.

On Thu, Jan 29, 2015 at 11:03 PM, Craig Silverman wrote:

Feed him many pints and collect excellent quotes!

On Thursday, January 29, 2015, Tom Phillips wrote:

BTW I'm in the pub with ███████ right now, we're having a chat about this.

On 29 Jan 2015 22:23, "Alan White" wrote:

So strange.

I've just claimed a couple more where Tanya may be able to help out because we have a geographic location. I think she's also going to see if there's someone in China who can search local media for her on some of the ones under my bit.

On Thu, Jan 29, 2015 at 10:16 PM, Craig Silverman wrote:

FYI I found two older penis choppings from CEN:

[2012] http://www.dailystar.co.uk/news/weird-news/263676/Man-has-penis-stolen-by-masked-intruders-after-alleged-affairs

[2008] http://www.dailystar.co.uk/news/weird-news/263676/Man-has-penis-stolen-by-masked-intruders-after-alleged-affairs

http://www.thesun.co.uk/sol/homepage/news/902117/China-Mother-kills-unfaithful-husband-Peng-Wang-chops-off-his-penis-and-shows-it-to-6-year-old-son-as-warning.html

Also found a third that is more recent and that I could confirm. It was from Mexico. this is so weird...

Craig

--

To: Michael Leidig
Subject: buzz

Michael, don't know if Buzzfeed have been on to you about this one. They have been on to our corporate comms again. Just wondered if you could let me have your take on the issues raised. Must admit am a bit bemused they are going after you again on a historic story. Aidan.

Dear Elizabeth,

I am working on a piece for BuzzFeed News about the story "'Drunk Santa and helper' in hospital facing drink drive charges after falling out of horse-drawn sleigh" published on the Mirror site on 23 December 2013. I have some questions regarding it:

1. Are you aware that two of the people quoted in this story deny ever saying the words attributed to them?

2. Are you aware that the "Santa" in the story, and his wife, were found by local authorities not to be drunk and claim their business and personal lives have been affected by the negative press coverage?

3. Are you aware a successful PCC complaint was made against the MailOnline and Huffington Post regarding this story?

4. Will you be issuing any corrections regarding it?

We're aiming to publish our story about this on Wednesday morning - I'd be grateful if you could get back to me by then. Please confirm receipt of request.

Best,

--

Alan White

News Reporter, BuzzFeed UK

AP01 (ef)

Appointment of Director

Company Name: **BuzzFeed UK Limited**

Company Number: **08318051**

Received for filing in Electronic Format on the: **10/12/2012**

New Appointment Details

Date of Appointment: 05/12/2012

Name: MARK FRACKT

Consented to Act: YES

Service Address: 54 WEST 21ST STREET
11TH FLOOR
NEW YORK
NY
USA
10010

Country/State Usually Resident: UNITED STATES

Date of Birth: 01/07/1977
Nationality: AMERICAN
Occupation: CFO BUZZFEED INC.

Printed in Great Britain
by Amazon

40941997R00077